PUFFIN BOOKS

What's **Black** & **White** & **Red** ALL Over?

What's **Black &** **White & Red** <u>ALL</u> Over?

Gyles Brandreth

PUFFIN

PUFFIN BOOKS

UK | USA | Canada | Ireland | Australia
India | New Zealand | South Africa

Puffin Books is part of the Penguin Random House group of companies
whose addresses can be found at global.penguinrandomhouse.com.

www.penguin.co.uk   www.puffin.co.uk   www.ladybird.co.uk

First published 2020

002

Text copyright © Gyles Brandreth, 2020
Illustrations copyright © Emily Fox, 2020

The moral right of the author and illustrator has been asserted

Text design by Mandy Norman
Printed in Great Britain by Clays Ltd, Elcograf S.p.A

A CIP catalogue record for this book is available from the British Library

ISBN: 978-0-241-42729-3

All correspondence to:
Puffin Books, Penguin Random House Children's
One Embassy Gardens, 8 Viaduct Gardens
London, SW11 7BW

Dedicated to my six best friends:
Rosa Carrots, Ivor Temper, Lydia Dustbin,
Constance Norah, Rani Nose and Lucy Lastick

CONTENTS

Chapter 1: Hello!   1

Chapter 2: Knock, knock! Come in!   19

Chapter 3: Meet the giraffes   35

Chapter 4: Here come the elephants   43

Chapter 5: Animal antics   59

Chapter 6: 'Waiter! Waiter!'   83

Chapter 7: Shaggy-dog stories   93

Chapter 8: A chapter of accidents   113

Chapter 9: Come into the library   131

Chapter 10: Verse and worse   161

Chapter 11: School jokes   177

Chapter 12: 'Doctor! Doctor!'   189

Chapter 13: Monster fun   203

Chapter 14: Silly riddles   221

Chapter 15: The best – and worst –   237
                jokes in the world

CHAPTER 1
HELLO!

My name is **GYLES BRANDRETH**

and I'm the JOKE BLOKE.

Yes, I'm the bloke with the jokes. I have been

collecting jokes for years. **AND YEARS**.

And now I want to share them with you.

These are the BEST JOKES I have ever come

across. AND THE WORST. Sometimes it's

difficult to tell the difference. In fact, often the

worst joke you've ever heard feels like the

BEST JOKE you've ever heard.

WHAT IS A JOKE?

Something that MAKES YOU LAUGH because it's **FUNNY**.

AND WHAT'S FUNNY?

Something that makes you **LAUGH**.

Of course, different people laugh at different things, but I hope that in the following pages you will find HUNDREDS OF **JOKES** that will make you **LAUGH**. There are jokes of every **SHAPE** and **SIZE**:

tall ones (about giraffes),

big ones (about elephants)

and **small ones** (about spiders).

There are jokes about **ghosts** and **ghoulies** – they're **spooktacular**!

There are jokes about going to the **moon** – they're OUT OF THIS WORLD.

There are jokes about going to **school** and going to the **DOCTOR**.

There are even JOKES about **JOKES**:

I told a **PANCAKE** a joke but it FELL FLAT.

A **BOXER** told me a joke.
The PUNCHLINE was a **KNOCKOUT**.

Have you heard the joke about the **BED**?
No?
It hasn't been **MADE UP** yet.

I would make jokes about the **SEA**,
but they're TOO DEEP.

An **ONION** just told me a joke.
I don't know whether to **LAUGH** or **CRY**.

Want to hear a joke about a

PIECE OF PAPER?

No?

Never mind . . . IT'S TEARABLE.

Get it? 'TEARABLE' sounds like **'TERRIBLE'**

– which is what that joke is. 'Tearable' means

something that can be torn, like a piece of

paper. Lots of the best jokes (and the worst

jokes) are based on **PUNS**.

What is a **PUN?**

A pun is a play on words – it uses words that

sound the same but have different meanings.

Why did the **SPIDER** go to the **COMPUTER?**

To check his **WEBSITE.**

The pun is on the word 'WEB':

spiders weave **WEBS** and you

find WEBSITES on the computer.

Why are **PLAYING CARDS** like **WOLVES?**

They come in PACKS.

A GROUP OF WOLVES is called A PACK,
and a set of playing cards is called a pack, too.

What was the REPORTER doing
at the **ICE-CREAM SHOP?**

Getting a SCOOP.

When reporters get an EXCLUSIVE NEWS
STORY, they call it a SCOOP. A ball of ice
cream is called a scoop, too.

He bought a **DONKEY** because he thought he
might get a KICK OUT OF IT.

To get a KICK OUT OF SOMETHING is to get
a THRILL OUT OF IT, and donkeys sometimes
use their hind legs to kick.

With some puns, the punning words SOUND
SIMILAR but they AREN'T EXACTLY
THE SAME.

What did the JUDGE say when the SKUNK

walked into the COURT ROOM?

'ODOUR IN THE COURT!'

Skunks give off a smell a bit like rotten eggs –

it's an UNPLEASANT ODOUR. The word

'odour' sounds a bit like the word 'order'. When

judges want to bring their courts to order they

say 'ORDER IN THE COURT!'

Here is another
SMELLY SKUNK joke:

Did you hear about the SKUNK that fell into

the river and STANK to the bottom?

Skunks STINK, so the pun is on 'stank',

which SOUNDS LIKE 'sank'.

I LOVE PUNS

because I love words

and the fun you can have with words.

I know puns about INSECTS really

BUG some people, but they don't

bother me. In fact, puns about BEES

give me a real **BUZZ**! I have a friend

who loves puns about BIRDS (yes,

TOUCAN play at this game!) and

another who laughs so much when she

hears a pun about SNAKES that she

has to **VIPER** way her tears.

Did you get that?

'Viper way' sounds like 'wipe away'.

ADDER NONSENSE, eh? Or should that be 'utter nonsense'? Now I have started on these snake puns, I can't stop. What do you get when you cross a SNAKE and a PIE? **A PIE-THON**! Pythons, adders and vipers are all types of snake, of course.

What's **PURPLE** and **GREEN** and
5,500 MILES LONG?
The GRAPE WALL OF CHINA.

Grapes are purple and green, and the
Great Wall of China is 5,500 miles long –
and about 2,700 years old.

Lots of jokes are also riddles, and lots of riddles
are also jokes.

What is a **RIDDLE**?

A riddle is a PUZZLING QUESTION with a funny, silly, clever or unexpected answer. Given the title of the book you are reading right now, you won't be surprised to learn that this is my all-time favourite:

What's **BLACK** and **WHITE** and **RED ALL OVER**?
The answer: **THIS BOOK!**

It's printed in black ink on white paper and by the time you have finished it, you will have read it all over! (At least, I hope you will have.)

Here is another version of the same riddle:

What's **BLACK** and **WHITE** and
RED ALL OVER?
A **NEWSPAPER**.

And here is another. The answer is sillier this time. (And funnier, I think.)

What's **BLACK** and **WHITE** and
RED ALL OVER?
A SUNBURNED ZEBRA.

That's what I love about jokes and riddles. They can be very **SILLY** indeed. If you stop to think about them, often they don't make sense. In fact, often they are nonsense. But I say, 'NONSENSE IS GOOD FOR YOU!'

Let's get sillier still.

What's **BLACK** and **WHITE**
and **RED ALL OVER?**
An **EMBARRASSED**
penguin.

What's **BLACK** and **WHITE** and
RED ALL OVER?
A **SKUNK** with **NAPPY RASH.**

What's **BLACK** and **WHITE** and
RED ALL OVER?
A chocolate-and-vanilla ice-cream sundae with
TOMATO KETCHUP poured all over it!

Riddles can be ridiculous, but sometimes they
can be clever, too.

What **BEGINS** with T, **ENDS** with T
and has T **INSIDE IT**?
A **TEAPOT**!

How many **BIRDS** can you put in
an **EMPTY CAGE**?
JUST ONE – after that the cage isn't empty!

JOKES CAN BE RIDDLES AND RIDDLES CAN BE JOKES.

You don't need to worry about the difference. In fact, with my **JOKE BOOK** I hope you won't have to worry about **ANYTHING**. We are just here to have **FUN**.

If you find any words in the book that you don't know the meaning of, look them up in a DICTIONARY or check them out online. I have included my own **DAFT** DICTIONARY in the book (page 144) – I hope it makes you chuckle. I have included LOTS OF MISTAKES, too – on purpose. They're collected together in a whole chapter of HOWLERS. There is another chapter of SHAGGY-DOG STORIES, and another full of **FUNNY POEMS**.

Don't worry if your job is small
And your rewards are few:
Remember that the MIGHTY OAK
*Was once a **NUT** like you!*

There is lots in here to make you laugh, and to make your family and friends laugh, too. There is nothing more fun than making other people laugh. But, when it comes to telling jokes, there *are* rules.

What are the **RULES**?

What's this? There are rules? This is supposed to be a joke book! THIS ISN'T A SCHOOL.

WHY ARE THERE RULES? 'Simples', as Orlov the meerkat in the TV adverts likes to say. Because if you want to be a successful joker, you need to know the rules. There are just seven of them, and here they are:

DO PRACTISE, PRACTISE, PRACTISE

before you tell a joke in public.

DO SPEAK CLEARLY without rushing what you're saying, and LOOK AT YOUR AUDIENCE when you are telling a joke.

DO CHOOSE THE RIGHT MOMENT to tell your joke. If your audience isn't in the right mood, even your funniest joke won't make them laugh.

DON'T

tell jokes that will hurt someone's feelings.

DON'T

start a joke unless you know how it finishes. The end – the PUNCHLINE, as it's called – is usually the best bit.

DON'T

tell the same joke to the same audience twice.

DON'T

tell a joke unless it's one that makes *you* laugh.
I hope that my jokes will make you **LAUGH**,
SMILE, GRIN, **TITTER**, SNIGGER, **CHUCKLE**,
CHORTLE, CACKLE, **GIGGLE**, GUFFAW,
HOOT, **ROAR** and roll around on the floor
biting the carpet in a happy state of helpless
merriment. You can *groan*, too, if the joke is a
really bad one. Welcome to the **WORST** – and
BEST – joke book in the world!

Now you're armed with your rules,
it's time to dive into the book. And
most importantly, have fun!

Gyles Brandreth
(The Joke Bloke)

CHAPTER 2
KNOCK, KNOCK!
COME IN!

Knock, knock!

Who's there?

ALEX.

Alex who?

ALEX PLAIN IF

YOU GIVE ME

HALF A CHANCE!

'KNOCK, KNOCK!'

jokes have been around for a very long time. The famous English playwright William Shakespeare first used the words 'Knock, knock! Who's there?' in his play *Macbeth* way back in the early 1600s, and people have been telling 'knock, knock' jokes of some kind for at least one hundred years.

As long ago as 1936, a company that made roofs for houses used a 'knock, knock' joke in a newspaper advertisement:

Knock, knock!

Who's there?

RUFUS.

Rufus who?

RUFUS the most important part of your house!

Do you see how the 'knock, knock' joke works?

The first two lines are always the same:

Knock, knock!

Who's there?

The next line has to be someone's or something's name, like Alex or Rufus – or Butter. The line after that is always the name followed by 'who?', so the final line can use the name again to lead you to the joke, like this:

Knock, knock!

Who's there?

BUTTER.

Butter who?

BUTTER let me in – I need the toilet!

The more unexpected the last line, the funnier the joke.

Knock, knock!

Who's there?

ISABEL.

Isabel who?

ISABEL NOT WORKING? I had to knock.

Knock, knock!

Who's there?

STAN.

Stan who?

STAN BACK, I'm going to sneeze!

Knock, knock!

Who's there?

ABBY.

Abby who?

ABBY BIRTHDAY to you,

ABBY BIRTHDAY to you,

ABBY BIRTHDAY, dear Abby,

ABBY BIRTHDAY TO YOU!

Knock, knock!

Who's there?

FRANK.

Frank who?

FRANK YOU for being my friend.

Knock, knock!

Who's there?

HOWARD.

Howard who?

HOWARD I KNOW?

Knock, knock!

Who's there?

KEN.

Ken who?

KEN I COME IN?

Knock, knock!

Who's there?

SHERLOCK.

Sherlock who?

SHERLOCK YOUR DOOR TIGHTLY SHUT, DON'T YOU?

Knock, knock!

Who's there?

CHEESE.

Cheese who?

CHEESE A NICE PERSON. Can I introduce you?

Knock, knock!

Who's there?

DOUGHNUT.

Doughnut who?

DOUGHNUT ASK, it's a secret!

Knock, knock!

Who's there?

ICE CREAM.

Ice cream who?

ICE CREAM if you don't let me inside!

Knock, knock!

Who's there?

LETTUCE.

Lettuce who?

LETTUCE IN – we're freezing out here!

Knock, knock!

Who's there?

LUKE.

Luke who?

LUKE THROUGH THE KEYHOLE TO SEE!

Knock, knock!

Who's there?

MIKEY.

Mikey who?

MIKEY DOESN'T FIT in the keyhole!

Knock, knock!

Who's there?

NANA.

Nana who?

NANA YOUR BUSINESS!

Knock, knock!

Who's there?

NOBEL.

Nobel who?

NO BELL, that's why I knocked!

Knock, knock!

Who's there?

WENDY.

Wendy who?

WENDY BELL WORKS AGAIN, I won't have to knock.

Knock, knock!

Who's there?

WILL.

Will who?

WILL YOU LET ME IN? I've been knocking for ages!

Knock, knock!

Who's there?

A HERD.

A herd who?

A HERD YOU WERE HOME,

how are you?

Knock, knock!

Who's there?

CHICK.

Chick who?

CHICK YOUR OVEN – I can smell burning!

Knock, knock!

Who's there?

DISHES.

Dishes who?

DISHES A NICE PLACE you've got here.

Knock, knock!

Who's there?

DOCTOR.

Doctor who?

Yes, and I brought a **DALEK** with me.

Knock, knock!

Who's there?

DOZEN.

Dozen who?

DOZEN ANYONE want to let me in?

Knock, knock!

Who's there?

HAL.

Hal who?

HAL YOU KNOW if you don't open the door?

Knock, knock!

Who's there?

NEEDLE.

Needle who?

NEEDLE LITTLE HELP getting in the door.

Knock, knock!

Who's there?

POLICE.

Police who?

POLICE MAY I COME IN?

Knock, knock!

Who's there?

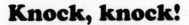

RADIO.

Radio who?

RADIO NOT, HERE I COME!

Knock, knock!

Who's there?

TANK.

Tank who?

YOU'RE WELCOME!

Knock, knock!

Who's there?

ARFER.

Arfer who?

ARFER GOT.

Knock, knock!

Who's there?

HOMER.

Homer who?

HOMER GAIN!

Knock, knock!

Who's there?

EWAN.

Ewan who?

NO ONE, JUST ME.

Knock, knock!

Who's there?

JUNO.

Juno who?

I DUNNO, d'you know?

Knock, knock!

Who's there?

HATCH.

Hatch who?

BLESS YOU!

Knock, knock!

Who's there?

DORIS.

Doris who?

DORIS JAMMED AGAIN.

Knock, knock!

Who's there?

Knock, knock!

Who's there?

Knock, knock!

Who's there?

Knock, knock!

Who's there?

Knock, knock!

Who's there?

I WISH YOU'D GET YOUR DOORBELL FIXED.

Knock, knock!

Who's there?

SOMEBODY WHO CAN'T REACH THE DOORBELL!

Knock, knock!

Who's there?

WOODEN SHOE.

Wooden shoe who?

WOODEN SHOE like to hear

another kind of joke?

YES!

And you can – right now . . .

CHAPTER 3
MEET THE GIRAFFES

What's a GIRAFFE'S favourite joke?
A **TALL** story.

What's a tall story? It's a story that's so

EXAGGERATED that it's very hard to believe.

Of course, it's the ridiculous exaggeration that

makes a tall story **FUNNY.**

HERE IS ONE

A boy went to the cinema and found a baby **GIRAFFE** sitting next to him in the front row.

'ARE YOU A BABY GIRAFFE?' ASKED THE BOY.

'I am,' said the **baby giraffe**.

'What are you doing here at the cinema?'

'The ice rink was closed, so I thought I'd come to the cinema for a change.'

AND HERE IS ANOTHER:

A girl took her pet GIRAFFE for a walk. It was a very long and **exhausting walk**.

On the way home, the girl and the GIRAFFE stopped at a cafe for a rest, a cup of tea and a piece of cake. After they'd had their tea and cake, the giraffe lay down on the floor of the cafe and fell asleep. The girl got up to leave.

'Hold on,' said the cafe owner. 'You can't just leave that LYING here.'

'That's not a **LION**, stupid,' said the girl.
'That's a giraffe!'

FUN FACTS

The giraffe is the TALLEST animal on earth.

Some giraffes are more than six metres tall.

Giraffes are vegetarians, which means they only eat plants. And fruit.

WHAT IS A GIRAFFE'S FAVOURITE FRUIT?
NECKtarines, of course!

In my book, some of the best jokes are GIRAFFE jokes.

Why does a giraffe have a long neck?

To connect its head to its body.

Why else does a giraffe have a long neck?

Because its FEET smell.

If a giraffe gets wet feet, will it develop a cold in the head?

Yes, but not until NEXT week.

Why do giraffes have small appetites?

Because a LITTLE goes a long way.

When is a baby giraffe taller than its mother?

When it sits on its father's shoulders.

What do giraffes have that no one else has?

BABY giraffes.

What do you call a giraffe that stands on your toe?

Anything you like, its head is too far away for it to **HEAR** you.

Why did the giraffe do badly at school?

He had his **HEAD** in the clouds.

When do giraffes have eight legs?

When there are **TWO GIRAFFES**.

What do you get when you cross a giraffe with a hedgehog?

A six-metre toothbrush.

Why are giraffes so slow to **apologize**?

*It takes them a **LONG** time*

to swallow their pride.

What do you call a giraffe driving a **fast** car

on the wrong side of the road?

Dangerous!

Did you hear about the race between the
giraffe and the **ostrich**?

It was neck and neck all the way.

Here is a YUCKY giraffe joke to finish with:
What's **green** and **hangs** from trees?

Giraffe **SNOT**.

Don't worry if your friends don't **LAUGH** at your giraffe jokes. They've probably gone **OVER** their heads.

CHAPTER 4

HERE
COME THE
ELEPHANTS

TEACHER: Name **six** wild animals

STUDENT: **FOUR** elephants and **TWO** giraffes.

What's worse than a **GIRAFFE**

with a **sore throat**?

An elephant with a **BLOCKED NOSE**!

Hickory, dickory, dock.

An elephant **RAN UP** the **clock** . . .

The clock is being **REPAIRED**.

FUN FACTS

Elephants are the world's LARGEST and HEAVIEST land animals.

There are **African** elephants and **Asian** elephants and it's easy to tell the difference: Asian elephants have STRAIGHTER backs and SMALLER ears.

ELEPHANTS may come from Africa and Asia, but elephant jokes were born in the UNITED STATES IN 1960. They quickly spread around the world.

How do you know if there's
an ELEPHANT in your oven?
You CAN'T SHUT *the door.*

How can you tell if an ELEPHANT'S
been in your fridge?
By the FOOTPRINTS *in the* **BUTTER**.

What's the difference between
a biscuit and an elephant?
You CAN'T DIP *an elephant in your tea.*

What's the difference between
an elephant and a postbox?
I don't know.
Well, I shan't send *you* **to post my letters.**

Why are ELEPHANTS so wrinkled?
Have you ever tried to iron one?

What's **green** and WRINKLY and has a long nose?

An elephant. I lied about the green part.

Why do ELEPHANTS paint their toenails **red**?

So they can hide in cherry trees.

I've **never** seen

an elephant in a cherry tree.

That shows it's a good disguise, doesn't it?

How does an elephant

get into a cherry tree?

It sits on a cherry stone and

WAITS FOR IT TO GROW.

How does an elephant

get out of a cherry tree?

It waits until autumn and

FLOATS DOWN *on a leaf.*

Why is an elephant LARGE,

grey and WRINKLED?

Because if it were small, red and juicy,

it would be a **STRAWBERRY**.

What did **Tarzan** say when he saw the **ELEPHANTS** coming?

'Here come the elephants.'

What did **TARZAN** say when he saw the elephants coming with **sunglasses** on?

Nothing, he didn't recognize them.

How do you get **FOUR ELEPHANTS** into a **Mini**?

Two in the FRONT and two in the BACK.

How do you get **FOUR HIPPOPOTAMUSES** into a **Mini**?

You can't, it's FULL OF ELEPHANTS.

What was the ELEPHANT

doing on the motorway?

About 5 mph.

Where does a TWO-TON elephant sleep?

ANYWHERE it wants to.

What did the river say

when the ELEPHANT sat in it?

'Well, I'M DAMMED.'

What do you have to know to

teach an elephant TRICKS?

MORE than the elephant.

Why can't two elephants

go swimming at the same time?

Because they only have one pair of

TRUNKS between them.

What do you give a **seasick** elephant?

Lots of room.

WHAT TIME is it when

an elephant sits on your **car**?

Time to get a NEW CAR.

What do you give a **nervous** elephant?

TRUNKquilizers.

Why did the elephants **leave** the circus?

They were tired of working for PEANUTS.

How do you **get down off** an elephant?

You don't, you get down off a DUCK.

Why do elephants have

wrinkled ANKLES?

They LACE UP their shoes too tightly.

How do you **scold** an elephant?

You say, 'TUSK, TUSK.'

What would happen if an elephant
SAT IN FRONT OF YOU at the cinema?

You'd MISS most of the film.

What's grey and stands in a river when
it **rains** without getting wet?

An elephant with an UMBRELLA.

There were **TWO ELEPHANTS** under
one umbrella. Why didn't they get wet?

It WASN'T raining.

What do you call an **ELEPHANT**
at the **North Pole**?

LOST!

What do you get if you cross

an elephant with a kangaroo?

GIANT HOLES all over AUSTRALIA.

Why couldn't the elephant ride a bicycle?

He didn't have THUMBS to ring the bell.

How do you stop an elephant

from smelling?

TIE A KNOT in its trunk.

What's the same SIZE and SHAPE as

an elephant but weighs nothing?

An elephant's SHADOW.

How is an elephant like a pineapple?

They are both large and grey.

Well, EXCEPT THE PINEAPPLE.

What is **LARGE** and **GREY** and wears **glass slippers**?

CINDERELEPHANT.

**What do you call an elephant that
never washes?**

A SMELLYphant!

What do you call two elephants on a bicycle?

Optimistic!

**What's the difference between an elephant
and a PIECE OF PAPER?**

*You can't make a PAPER AEROPLANE
out of an elephant.*

**What's the difference between a
lemon and an elephant?**

A lemon is YELLOW.

**What's the difference between
a flea and an ELEPHANT?**

*An elephant CAN HAVE fleas
but a flea CAN'T have elephants.*

How do you get an elephant

INTO **a matchbox**?

You take out the matches first.

What do you get when you

cross a **whale** with an ELEPHANT?

VERY BIG swimming trunks.

What is **grey** and has

FOUR LEGS and a TRUNK?

A mouse GOING on a long

holiday in the sun.

What is **brown** and has

FOUR LEGS and a TRUNK?

A mouse COMING BACK from

a long holiday in the sun.

Those were MOUSE JOKES, not
ELEPHANT JOKES. Time to join the
rest of the animals . . .

CHAPTER 5
ANIMAL ANTICS

This next joke is probably the **oldest joke** there is about an animal. EVERYONE knows it.

Why did the CHICKEN cross the road?

To get to the OTHER SIDE.

HAHA!

There are DIFFERENT VERSIONS of the famous chicken joke, like this one:

Why did the chicken cross the road?

To show everyone he WASN'T CHICKEN.

AND THIS ONE:

Why did the turkey cross the road?

To prove he wasn't chicken EITHER!

FUN FACTS

People have been using the word 'chicken' to mean 'cowardly' for hundreds of years.

English playwright **WILLIAM SHAKESPEARE** – he keeps popping up because he loved playing with words – used 'chicken' to mean 'cowardly' in one of his plays back in the 1600s.

SIXTY-SIX MILLION YEARS before Shakespeare's time, dinosaurs roamed the earth.

And why did the dinosaur cross the road? *The chicken WASN'T AROUND yet.*

**Here is a 'CHICKEN CROSSING THE ROAD'
joke that's actually about a COW.**

(If you don't like it, feel free to **moo**!)

Why did the COW cross the road?

Because the chicken was on HOLIDAY.

This one is **JUST ABOUT A COW**:

Why did the COW cross the road?

To get to the UDDER SIDE.

And this one is **ABOUT A SHEEP**:

Why did the SHEEP cross the road?

To get to the BAA-BAA SHOP!

In the world of ANIMAL JOKES, animals come in all shapes and sizes. Some are **FARM ANIMALS**, some are wild animals, some are HUGE and some are SMALL. Some have feathers, some have scales. Some are even extinct, like the dinosaur from earlier . . . and these ones:

What's it called when a dinosaur crashes its car?

A Tyrannosaurus WRECK!

What does a triceratops sit on?

Its tricera-BOTTOM!

What do you get when you cross a pig with a dinosaur?

Jurassic PORK.

What do you call a dinosaur that is sleeping?

A dino-SNORE!

FUN FACTS

The **BLUE WHALE** is the **LARGEST** ANIMAL of all time known to have existed. It can reach a weight of about **180 tons** and a length of around **30 metres**. A blue whale's tongue can weigh as much as an **ENTIRE ELEPHANT** – and that's no joke.

Where do you weigh whales?

At the WHALE-WEIGH station.

65

What do you call an **untidy** HIPPOPOTAMUS?

*A hippopota-**MESS**.*

What's a CROCODILE'S favourite **card game?**

SNAP.

What do you call a FISH **without** an eye?

Fsh!

What do you do if your dog CHEWS **a dictionary?**

Take the WORDS out of its mouth.

What goes TICK-TOCK, **woof-woof,** TICK-TOCK, **woof-woof?**

A WATCH DOG.

What do you call a **COW** that eats your **grass?**

A LAWN MOO-ER.

What is a SNAKE'S favourite subject at school?

HISS-tory.

Why does a dog wag its tail?

Because there's NO ONE ELSE to wag it for him.

How do you make a GOLDFISH old?

Take away the 'G'.

How does a MOUSE feel after it takes a shower?

SQUEAKY clean!

What has four legs and goes 'Oom, Oom'?

A cow going BACKWARDS!

What do you call a PIG that's been
arrested for dangerous driving?

A ROAD HOG.

What does a cat say when
somebody STEPS ON ITS TAIL?

'ME-OW!'

What do you call a DEER with no eyes?

NO-EYE DEER!

How do you stop a dog barking
in the BACK SEAT of a car?

Put him in the FRONT seat.

What was the FIRST ANIMAL in space?

The COW that JUMPED OVER THE MOON.

Where do FISH keep their MONEY?

In a RIVERBANK!

What is the easiest way to
count a **HERD OF CATTLE?**

With a COW-culator.

What do you get from a **BAD-TEMPERED shark?**

As far away as possible.

There were **TWO COWS** in a field.
One of the cows said, **'MOO!'** and the other
one said, **'That's just what I was going to say.'**

How many **skunks** does it take
to make a **BIG STINK?**

A PHEW.

Why **DON'T** bears wear **shoes?**

What's the POINT? They'd still have BEAR FEET.

What do you call a **dog** that likes **BUBBLE BATHS?**

A SHAM-poodle!

What do you give a pig with a RASH?

OINKment.

What do you do if your CAT

swallows your PENCIL?

Use a PEN.

What do you call a snake with

NO CLOTHES on?

SNAKED.

What did the DOG say to the flea?

'Stop BUGGING me!'

What do camels use to HIDE themselves?

CAMELflage.

What did the PORCUPINE say to the CACTUS?

'Is that you, Mum?'

What is a frog's favourite YEAR?

A LEAP year.

What is a HORSE'S favourite sport?

STABLE tennis.

**How many sheep do you need
to make a SWEATER?**

I don't know. I didn't think sheep could knit.

Which ANIMAL can't be TRUSTED?

A CHEETah.

**If a quadruped has FOUR feet and a
biped has TWO feet, what is a zebra?**

A STRI-PED.

**Why are FOUR-LEGGED animals
such bad dancers?**

Because they have TWO LEFT FEET.

What do you call a **PONY** with a sore throat?

A LITTLE HOARSE.

'My horse is very **polite**. When he comes to a fence he stops to **LET ME GO OVER FIRST.**'

What did the horse say when he got to **THE END** of his **nosebag**?

'This is the LAST STRAW.'

How do you fit **MORE PIGS** on your farm?

*Build a **STY**SCRAPER!*

What did the **farmer** call the cow that **DIDN'T MAKE MILK?**

An UDDER failure.

What do you get from a **pampered** cow?

SPOILED milk.

Why do fish live in SALTWATER?

*Because **PEPPER**WATER would*

make them SNEEZE!

How do LIONS GREET

other animals in the savannah?

'Pleased to EAT you.'

What happened to the lion
when it ATE THE CLOWN?

It felt all FUNNY INSIDE.

Which fish only swims at NIGHT?

A STARfish.

Why is a fish EASY to weigh?

Because it has its OWN SCALES!

Which animal is OUT OF BOUNDS?

An EXHAUSTED KANGAROO!

What did the **buffalo** say to **HIS SON**

when he went away on a trip?

'**BI**SON!'

What do you call a **BEAR** with **NO EARS?**

B.

Why wouldn't the **PIGLETS** listen to their **FATHER?**

*Because he was such an OLD **BOAR**.*

What do you call **pigs** who **LIVE TOGETHER?**

PEN friends.

First sheep: BAA-AA-AA-AA.
Second sheep: MOO.

First sheep: What do you mean, "MOO"?
Second sheep: I'm learning a **foreign language**.

Why is it hard to talk with a **GOAT** around?

Because it always BUTTS in.

How does an **OCTOPUS** go into battle?

Well ARMED.

What did the **BEAVER** say to the **TREE**?

'It was nice GNAWING you.'

What's **ANOTHER NAME** for a water otter?

A kettle.

What did the **DOG** say when it **SAT**
on the **SANDPAPER**?

'ROUGH.'

What happened to the **cat** that
SWALLOWED a ball of **WOOL**?

She had MITTENS.

What do you call a CAT that sucks LEMONS?

A **SOUR**PUSS.

Who tells CHICKEN JOKES?

Comedi-HENS.

How do you tell which END of a
WORM is the HEAD?

Tickle its MIDDLE and see which end SMILES.

What's the BIGGEST ant in the world?

A GI**ANT**.

Why do bees HUM?

Because they DON'T KNOW the words.

What did the mother bee say to
the NAUGHTY baby bee?

'BEEHIVE yourself.'

How do **BEES** get to **SCHOOL?**

By school BUZZ!

What did one flea **SAY** to the other?

'Shall we WALK or TAKE A DOG?'

What do you call a **DOG MAGICIAN?**

A LABRACADABRADOR.

What do you call an **alligator** that **SOLVES MYSTERIES?**

An investiGATOR.

What steps should you take if a tiger is **RUNNING towards** you?

Big ones AWAY from it!

What is more **AMAZING** than a **talking dog?**

A SPELLING BEE.

A team of SMALL **ANIMALS** and a team of **BIG ANIMALS** decided to play football. During the first half of the game, the big animals were winning two–nil, but during the second half a **centipede** came on to the pitch and scored **SO MANY GOALS** that the small animals won the game.

When it was over, the captain of the big animals' team (who was a **gorilla**) asked the centipede, 'Where were you during the **FIRST HALF**?'

The centipede answered,
'Putting on my boots.'

Before we leave our **AMAZING menagerie**, here are some jokes about MIXING UP **REAL** animals to CREATE funny **IMAGINARY** ones. These joke animals don't exist, but wouldn't it be fun if they did?

What do you get if you cross a giraffe with a DOG?

An animal that BARKS at LOW-FLYING aeroplanes.

What do you get if you cross a BEAR with a kangaroo?

*A FUR COAT with **POCKETS**.*

What do you get if you cross a SHEEPDOG with a jellyfish?

CollieWOBBLES.

What do you get when you
cross a **sheepdog** with a **DAFFODIL?**

A *COLLIE-FLOWER.*

What do you get if you
cross a **DOG** with a **vegetable?**

A *JACK BRUSSEL.*

What do you get when you cross
a **HAMMOCK** with a **dog?**

A *ROCKER spaniel.*

What do you get if you cross
a **COW** with a **camel?**

LUMPY milkshakes.

**What do you get if you cross
a PIG with a zebra?!**

Striped sausages.

**What do you get if you cross
a chicken with a POODLE?**

POOCHED eggs.

**What do you get if you cross a
CARRIER PIGEON with a woodpecker?**

*A bird that KNOCKS before it
delivers a message.*

CHAPTER 6

'WAITER! WAITER!'

**Did you hear about the
NEW RESTAURANT on the MOON?**
Great food but NO ATMOSPHERE.

There are lots of RESTAURANTS, CAFES
and COFFEE SHOPS in the world of jokes.
Lots of **CUSTOMERS**, too, which is odd because
they always seem to be complaining – mostly
about the **SOUP** . . .

'Waiter, waiter, there's a **FLY** in my **SOUP**!'

'It's all right, madam, IT CAN SWIM.'

'Waiter, waiter, there's a **FLY** in my **SOUP**!'

'Don't worry, sir, the SPIDER ON YOUR ROLL
will catch it.'

'Waiter, waiter, there's a **FLY** in my **SOUP**!'

'I'm sorry, madam, I didn't realize you
wished to DINE ALONE.'

'Waiter, waiter, there's a **FLY** in my **SOUP**!'

'No, sir, that's a COCKROACH.
The fly is on your steak.'

'Waiter, waiter, there's a **FLY** in my **SOUP**!'

'Not so loud, madam, or they'll ALL be wanting one.'

'Waiter, waiter, there's a FLY in my **SOUP**!'
*'It's OK, sir, there's NO **EXTRA** CHARGE.'*

'Waiter, waiter, there's a FLY in my **SOUP**!'
'So sorry, madam. I must have missed it when I removed the other three.'

Over the years, the original **'FLY IN MY SOUP'** joke has developed a few variations.

'Waiter, what's this FLY doing in my **SOUP**?'
'The breaststroke, sir.'

'Waiter, what is THIS **SOUP**?'
'It's BEAN soup, madam.'
'I don't care what it's **BEEN**, what is it **NOW**?'

'Waiter, there's **NO CHICKEN**
in this **CHICKEN SOUP**.'

'No, sir, and there aren't any shepherds
in the SHEPHERD'S PIE either.'

'Waiter, there's a **FLEA** in my **SOUP!**'

'Shall I tell him to HOP it?'

'Waiter, there's a **DEAD FLY** in my **SOUP!**'

'Yes, sir, it's the HOT WATER that **KILLS** them.'

'Waiter, there's a **DEAD FLY** in my **SOUP!**'

'What did you expect for £2.50 – a LIVE one?'

'Waiter, there is a dead fly

SWIMMING in my **SOUP**!'

'*Don't be silly, DEAD FLIES CAN'T SWIM.*'

'Waiter, what's this **FLY** doing in my **SOUP**?'

'*What did you expect? It's FLY SOUP!*'

'Waiter, there's a **BEE** in my **SOUP**.'

'*Yes, sir, it's the FLY'S DAY OFF.*'

'Waiter, this plate is **WET**.'

'*That's THE SOUP, madam.*'

WAITER JOKES have many different versions. There are even some that START with the waiter speaking.

'How did you **FIND** your **STEAK**, sir?'
'*With a MAGNIFYING GLASS.*'

'We have practically **EVERYTHING** on the **MENU**, madam.'
'*So I see. Will you bring me A CLEAN ONE, please?*'

'What will you have to **FOLLOW** the **ROAST CHICKEN**, sir?'
'*Indigestion, I expect.*'

Unfortunately, however hard **THE WAITERS** try to please their customers, they DON'T seem to succeed.

'Waiter, I'm in a hurry.
Will my **OMELETTE** be **LONG**?'

'No, madam, it will be ROUND,
like everybody else's.'

'Waiter, do they **EVER CHANGE** the **TABLECLOTHS** in this establishment?'

'I don't know, sir, I've only
worked here FOR A YEAR.'

'Waiter, bring me a **BURNT** sausage, a pile of **GREASY** chips and a **LEATHERY** egg.'

'Oh, I couldn't possibly serve you
food like that, madam.'

'Why not? **YOU DID YESTERDAY**.'

'Waiter, there's a **BUTTON** in my $\mathbf{SALAD}$.'

'Yes, sir. It must have fallen off while the salad was getting DRESSED.'

'Waiter, do you **SERVE CRABS**?'

'Sit down. WE SERVE ANYBODY.'

'There's only **ONE PIECE** of $\mathbf{MEAT}$ on my plate, waiter.'

'One moment, sir, I'll CUT IT IN TWO.'

'Waiter, I can't eat this **DREADFUL FOOD. Call the manager.**'

'It's no use, sir. HE WON'T EAT IT EITHER.'

'Waiter, waiter, there's $\mathbf{SOAP}$ in this food.'

'That's to WASH IT DOWN with, madam.'

'Waiter, this **LEMONADE** is all **CLOUDY**.'

'*The lemonade is fine, sir,*

it's just the GLASS that's DIRTY.'

'Waiter, a cup of tea **WITHOUT MILK**, please.'

'*I'm sorry, sir, WE'RE OUT OF MILK.*

Will you have it WITHOUT sugar?'

'Waiter, would you please get your

thumb **OUT** of my **SOUP**?'

'*So sorry, madam, but I have A BOIL on my*

thumb and the doctor told me to keep it warm.'

'Waiter, this soup **TASTES FUNNY**.'

'*Then why aren't you LAUGHING?*'

'Waiter, there is a **FLY** in the **BUTTER**!'

'*Yes, sir, it's a BUTTERfly!*'

'Waiter, there is a **CATERPILLAR**
in my **SALAD**!'

*'I'm sorry, madam, I didn't know you
were a VEGETARIAN.'*

'Waiter, what's **WRONG** with these **EGGS**?'

'I don't know, sir, I only LAID THE TABLE.'

'Waiter, how **LONG** have you **WORKED** here?'

'Only two weeks, madam. Why?'

'You can't be the one who
TOOK MY ORDER then.'

Waiter: '**TEA** or **COFFEE**?'

First customer: 'I'll have tea.'

Second customer: 'Me, too – and make
sure the cup is **CLEAN**.'

(The waiter leaves, then returns.)

Waiter: 'Two teas. Which one of you
asked for the **CLEAN CUP**?'

CHAPTER 7
SHAGGY-DOG STORIES

Shaggy-dog stories are LONG STORIES that don't really lead anywhere – except to a last line that's either a bit of a **DAMP SQUIB** (like a firework that doesn't go off) or a funny PLAY ON WORDS. The original shaggy-dog story is over a hundred years old, and it goes like this:

SHAGGY
THE
SHAGGY-DOG

ONCE UPON A TIME there was a boy called Ben who had a long-haired dog called **Shaggy**. (Shaggy didn't know his name was Shaggy. Shaggy thought his name was 'DOWN BOY'.) Ben was so proud that Shaggy was so long-haired and that he looked so **shaggy** that he entered him in the village's shaggy-dog contest – and Shaggy won. Ben was excited and delighted. Next, he decided to enter Shaggy in the **SHAGGY-DOG CONTEST** in the nearby big town. Shaggy won that, too.

Thrilled, Ben decided to enter Shaggy in the **NATIONAL SHAGGY-DOG CONTEST** – Shaggy won that competition as well. Finally, Ben decided to enter Shaggy in the world shaggy-dog championships. It was a major international event held in New York City, USA. When the judges had inspected all of the competing dogs, one of them looked at Shaggy and said, 'He's **NOT THAT SHAGGY**, is he?'

* * *

Here are **SOME MORE** shaggy-dog stories. These aren't about shaggy-dogs, but they are still quite **silly**. You can take as long as you like when you tell them. That's the point of a shaggy-dog story. You are supposed to **SPIN THE STORY OUT** – and your audience is supposed to **groan** when you reach the last line. With these stories, you can be sure they will!

THE FISHERMAN'S TWO SONS

THIS IS A SAD STORY, but it's true. Once upon a time, a long time ago, on a lonely island in the middle of the sea, there lived a **FISHERMAN**.

The fisherman was called **Up** and his wife was called **Down**. (Funny names, I know, but there you go. It's a funny old world.) Every morning Up, the fisherman, went out in his boat to catch as many fish as he could, and every evening when he came home, no matter how many wonderful fish he had caught, no matter how big they were, he would tell his family of the amazing monster-sized fish he had seen and **ALMOST** caught.

The fisherman had two sons. One was called **Towards** and the other was called **Away**. Eventually the day dawned when Up and Down's sons were big enough to go out fishing with Up for the first time. When he returned that evening, he was **VERY** UPSET.

'Down, my dear,' he said to his wife, 'you wouldn't believe the huge fish we saw today. It was over five metres long, and it came up to the boat, **REACHED** up over the side, and it grabbed Towards and swallowed him WHOLE!'

'Oh, no!' cried Down. 'How terrible! Oh, poor, dear Towards!'

'I'm afraid that's only half the story,' said the fisherman, **SHAKING** his head sadly. 'You should have seen the one that got **Away**.'

THE
TORTOISE
FAMILY

Tortoises, sloths, snails and starfish are among the **SLOWEST** animals on earth. This story could be about a family of starfish or snails or sloths, but it is about a family of tortoises who went into a cafe for some ice cream.

FATHER TORTOISE ordered **VANILLA** ice cream, Mother Tortoise ordered **STRAWBERRY** ice cream, and little Tommy Tortoise ordered **CHOCOLATE** ice cream. The family were just about to start eating their ice creams when Father Tortoise said, 'I think it's going to rain. Would you pop home, please, Tommy, and fetch my **umbrella**?'

Off went Tommy. Three days later he still hadn't returned. 'I think,' said Mother Tortoise to Father Tortoise, 'that we had better eat Tommy's ice cream before it melts.' A voice from just by the cafe door called out, **'IF YOU DO THAT I won't GO!'**

HAVE A
BANANA

ONCE UPON A TIME, a long while ago, in the early days of the railways, two old gentlemen, **Gabriel** and **Thomas**, were persuaded to take a train to the big city to visit some of their relatives. Neither of them had ever left their village before. Because it was a long journey, a kind friend had given them a BUNCH OF BANANAS to eat on the way. They had never eaten bananas before, either.

They travelled along for a while, marvelling at the **SPEED** of the train and watching the trees and the countryside flash past. Then, they began to feel a bit PECKISH.

'Try one of these bananas,' said Gabriel to Thomas.

'I don't mind if I do,' said Thomas to Gabriel.

Just as Thomas took a **BITE** of his banana, the train entered a tunnel. 'Have you eaten your banana yet?' he called out.

'No,' said Gabriel.

'Well, don't touch it,' cried Thomas. 'I took one bite and went **blind**.'

LITTLE
LUCY

LITTLE LUCY'S PARENTS had invited Mr and Mrs Smith-Jones over to their house for dinner. They arrived early and Lucy's parents were busy in the KITCHEN, so little **Lucy** went into the living room to entertain the guests.

Looking at little Lucy, Mrs Smith-Jones whispered to her husband, 'She isn't very **P-R-E-T-T-Y**, is she?' SPELLING out the word.

'Perhaps not,' answered little Lucy in a loud, clear voice, 'but she is quite **B-R-I-G-H-T**.'

HOW TO
CAPTURE A
CROCODILE

ANYBODY CAN CAPTURE A CROCODILE. This is how you go about it. First, get a telescope, a matchbox, a pair of tweezers and a **large**, LONG, very **boring** BOOK.

Next, choose a STEAMY hot day and go down to the riverbank where the crocodiles live. Just sit down, with the telescope, the matchbox and the tweezers next to you, and start to read your large, long, very boring book. Because the book is **so** BORING and the day is so hot, you will fall asleep quite quickly.

Once you are asleep, a crocodile will see you and, naturally, it will come over to investigate. It will **PEER** over your shoulder at the book and start to read. Because the day is so hot and the book is **SO** BORING, the crocodile will fall asleep quite quickly, too.

When the crocodile has **DROPPED OFF**, you wake up. As soon as you do, pick up your telescope and look through the WRONG END at the crocodile. The crocodile will now look **VERY SMALL**, so you can use your tweezers to pick him **UP** and put him into your matchbox. And there you have YOUR CROCODILE.

TWO BOYS
IN THE
GRAVEYARD

ONE AUTUMN EVENING, Bill and Will went out to collect CONKERS. They collected a huge bag, then decided to go and share them out in the graveyard. Just as they walked through the gates into the graveyard, two conkers rolled out of the bag. 'We'll get those later,' said Bill. 'Let's go and share out the others first.'

As they were sharing the conkers out, an **OLD LADY** walked across the graveyard taking a shortcut home. To her **horror**, she could hear voices saying, 'One for you, one for me, one for you, one for me . . .' through the darkness. She flew to the gate in a terrible state, where she bumped straight into a passing police officer.

'What's the matter, madam?' he asked, seeing the poor old lady was **TREMBLING** with fear.

'Oh,' she wailed, 'there are **ghosts** in the graveyard, and they're sharing out the dead bodies. Listen.' The old woman and the police officer stood still. A voice floated out to them on the night air: 'One for you, one for me, and we mustn't forget **THOSE TWO BY THE GATE**.'

THE TALKING
HIPPOPOTAMUS

ONE HOT SUNNY DAY a hippopotamus strolled into a cafe and ordered a large orange juice with ice. The waiter was **amazed** to see the hippo and to hear him speak, but he served him the glass of orange juice. The hippo **DRAINED** the orange juice and sucked the ice cubes, then silently handed the waiter a five-pound note. The waiter, thinking that the hippo would know nothing about money, decided to cheat him and handed him ONE POUND IN CHANGE. 'I hope you enjoyed the orange juice,' the waiter said. 'It's not often we get hippos in here, you know.'

'With orange juice at **FOUR POUNDS A GLASS**, I'm not surprised,' replied the hippo.

THE MAGICIAN
AND THE
PARROT

THE **SS** *LUXURIANA* was a large cruise ship. It spent the whole year travelling the seas and oceans of the world carrying people on luxury cruises. The ship had wonderfully comfortable cabins, beautiful restaurants and an on-board theatre where shows were put on to entertain the passengers every night. Among the many performers working in the ship's theatre was a VERY **CLEVER magician**. This magician could do all sorts of extraordinary tricks: he could **SAW** people in half, produce **RABBITS FROM HATS** and, best of all, make things DISAPPEAR before your very eyes.

One of the sailors on the ship had a **parrot**, and the parrot took a great DISLIKE to the magician. Every time the magician performed his act, the parrot would squawk, **'PHONEY, PHONEY!'**

Unhappily, the day came when DISASTER struck the SS *Luxuriana*. In a terrible storm, the cruise ship hit some hidden rocks and **SANK** without trace. All that remained was one lifeboat and the only SURVIVORS of the disaster were the magician and the parrot. The parrot sat at one end of the lifeboat and the magician sat at the other. For two whole days, neither the parrot nor the magician spoke a word. Finally, the parrot sighed, then turned to the magician and said, 'I give up. **WHAT DID YOU DO WITH THE SHIP**?'

A HORSE'S TALE

ONCE UPON A TIME, a man went to an auction sale to buy a **horse**. He found a beautiful animal that seemed to be just what he'd wanted, but it was very cheap. 'Is there anything wrong with this horse?' he asked the horse dealer. 'It's a low price for such a good-looking animal.'

'There's just one small thing,' said the dealer. 'He likes to sit down on **BANANAS**. Whenever he sees one, he goes and sits on it and refuses to move.'

'He's not likely to see many bananas where I live,' said the man. 'I think I'll buy him.'

So the man paid for the horse, got on it and set off for home. On the way, he had to cross a stream on his horse. Right in the very MIDDLE of the stream, the horse sat down and the man slid off. *There must be a banana in this stream*, thought the man. He waded through the water, looking all around the horse, but he couldn't see anything that resembled a banana. He pulled at the horse's bridle and urged it on, but the horse just sat there and refused to move.

After a while the man gave up. He **CLIMBED OUT** of the stream. Soaking wet and **VERY ANGRY**, he made his way back to the auction to find the dealer who had sold him the horse. **'Oi!'** he shouted when he got there. 'That horse you sold me. You said the only thing wrong with it was that it sat on bananas. But it sat down in the middle of a stream where there were no bananas. I've tried everything and I can't get it to move!'

'Oh dear,' said the dealer. 'I forgot to tell you. **IT SITS ON fish, TOO.'**

CHAPTER 8
A CHAPTER OF
ACCIDENTS

Welcome to a chapter of accidents.

It's packed with HILARIOUS **HOWLERS**,

CLASSIC **CLANGERS**, GLORIOUS GAFFES and

brilliant **BLUNDERS**, BOTCHES, **BLOOMERS**,

BLOOPERS and **BOOBOOS**.

They're all things that people have seen,

said or written that are jockey by mistake.

OOPS – *JOKEY* by mistake!

SCHOOLROOM STINKERS

We all make mistakes, especially when we're at skool. Sorry, *SCHOOL*. Here are some real howlers reported by real teachers who claim that these real mistakes were made by real kids in real schools. (If you can, try to work out what the students *SHOULD* have written or said.)

ANCIENT EGYPT was inhabited by mummies and they all wrote in **HYDRAULICS**.

THE GREEKS were a highly sculptured people, and without them we wouldn't have history. The Greeks also had myths. A MYTH is a **FEMALE MOTH**.

SOCRATES was a famous Greek teacher who went around giving people advice. Sadly, Socrates died from an overdose of **WEDLOCK**.

IT WAS AN AGE of great inventions and discoveries. Gutenberg invented the Bible. Sir Walter Raleigh invented the **POTATO**.

JOAN OF ARC was married to NOAH. She was burnt to a **STEAK** a long time ago.

Q: Name the FOUR SEASONS.
A: Salt, pepper, mustard and **VINEGAR**.

THE CLIMATE of the SARAH is so hot that the people have to live somewhere else. They travel by **CAMELOT**.

THE PYRAMIDS are a range of MOUNTAINS between France and Spain.

MADMAN CURIE discovered **RADIO**.

KING HENRY VIII couldn't walk because he had an **ABBESS** on each knee.

The FRENCH NATIONAL ANTHEM is called the **MAYONNAISE**.

When your EYES NEED TESTING you go to an **OPTIMIST**.

PEOPLE who live to be ONE HUNDRED become **CENTURIONS**.

TELEPATHY is a code invented by **SAMUEL MORSE**.

The inhabitants of PARIS
are called **PARASITES**.

An **OXYGEN** has EIGHT SIDES.

REEFS are what you put on COFFINS.

A HOSTAGE is a nice person who
LOOKS AFTER YOU on an aeroplane.

LOUIS PASTEUR found the CURE FOR
RABBITS.

A STOWAWAY is the person with the
BIGGEST **APPETITE** on a ship.

The **SEWAGE CANAL** is in Egypt.

NEWSPAPER HEADLINES

The trouble with **WRITING A HEADLINE** for a newspaper is that you only have a small space in which to fit the words to tell readers what a story is all about. This means that sometimes things can go a bit **WRONG**.

PASSENGERS HIT BY CANCELLED TRAINS

POLICE FOUND SAFE UNDER BLANKET

MAGISTRATES ACT TO KEEP THEATRE OPEN

STUDENTS COOK AND SERVE GRANDPARENTS

THIRTY-YEAR FRIENDSHIP ENDS AT ALTAR

**PROTESTER TRIED TO SPOIL PLAY
BUT THE ACTORS SUCCEEDED**

MAN FOUND DEAD IN GRAVEYARD

Sometimes, newspapers make **MISTAKES** with
MISPRINTS – they get a word wrong by leaving
out a letter or printing the wrong letter.

OFFICER CONVICTED OF ACCEPTING BRIDE

**WEATHER FORECAST:
A DEPRESSION WILL MOPE ACROSS ENGLAND**

TOURISTS HEAD FOR SEA AND SIN

**TOWN TO HAVE PARENT–TEACHER
ASSASSINATION**

**MAN ADMITTED TO HOSPITAL
SUFFERING FROM BUNS**

SLIPS OF THE TONGUE

Sometimes we **DON'T SAY EXACTLY** what we mean. Or we say what we think we mean, but it doesn't sound quite right – like the dad who said to his son as the boy took his third apple from the bowl:

'Apples DON'T GROW on **TREES**, son.'

Here are some **MORE** slips of the tongue:

'If you don't come back,
I shan't let you **GO AGAIN**.'

'If my grandfather were **ALIVE**,
he'd turn over in his **GRAVE**.'

'In a word – I DON'T THINK SO.'

'**KEEP QUIET** when you're SPEAKING to me!'

SIGN OF THE
TIMES

These are REAL SIGNS that have been spotted

in an assortment of public places.

IN A **COUNTRY LANE**:

When this sign is UNDERWATER

the ROAD IS CLOSED to traffic.

ON A **VILLAGE GREEN**:

It is FORBIDDEN to throw stones at

THIS NOTICE.

OUTSIDE A **SCHOOL**:

SLOW

CHILDREN

CROSSING

AT A **RAILWAY STATION**:

TOILETS OUT OF ORDER.

Please USE platforms 5 and 6.

AT A **BUS STATION**:

TOILETS

ONLY

FOR

PREGNANT

ELDERLY

CHILDREN

ON **SOUTHEND PIER:**

DON'T THROW

PEOPLE BELOW

AT THE **ROADSIDE:**

Caution. Men at work. Dead slow.

AT A **WILDFOWL CENTRE:**

QUIET

BIRDS HAVE EARS

ON AN **ELECTRICITY PYLON:**

Danger! Touching these wires will result

IN INSTANT DEATH. Anyone found doing so

will be PROSECUTED.

IN AN **OFFICE KITCHEN**:

STAFF should empty teapots and then stand
UPSIDE DOWN on the draining board.

OUTSIDE A **WORKSHOP**:

Installers of central heating and
plumbing for fourteen years.
A. C. PUDDLE & CO. LTD

IN A **DEPARTMENT STORE**:

Bargain basement UPSTAIRS.

IN A **DRY-CLEANING SHOP**:

CUSTOMERS leaving garments more than
thirty days will be DISPOSED of.

IN A **SHOP WINDOW**:

Why shop elsewhere and be CHEATED
when you CAN COME HERE?

IN A **CAFE**:

Customers who find OUR STAFF RUDE
should wait and SEE THE MANAGER.

AT A **SCHOOL**:

Will the person who borrowed a LADDER
from the caretaker please return it immediately
or FURTHER STEPS will be taken.

AT A **FARM**:

HORSE MANURE

Filled bag – £2

Do-it-yourself – £3

TERRIBLE
TRANSLATIONS

Understanding **OTHER LANGUAGES**
isn't easy, and it's very easy to make
MISTAKES. Someone I know once went
on holiday to Greece and spent two weeks
greeting everyone there with the word
'**SQUID**' (*kalamari*) instead of
'**GOOD MORNING**' (*kalimera*).

Here are some dishes that might be offered
in restaurants where the English translation on
the menu isn't quite correct:

SOAP of the day

FIZZ soup

HAND and egg

FRIGHTENED **EEGS**

SAUCEAGE EEG AN CHAPS
speciality of the HOWS

flush of young DEAR, MUCHROOMS,
OBJERJEANS, in white **WHINE** SORTS,
all cooked up in your SEAT

BOLED EEGS IN CREME **SORES**

SURPRISED chicken

rice **HASHED**

roast **PEASANT** in cream sauce

ANGRY duck in orange SORTS

COUGHEE EGGSPRESS

Now for some NOTICES to guests found in hotels AROUND THE WORLD.

In the event of fire, the visitor, avoiding panic, is to walk down the corridor and **WARM** the chambermaid.

After the typhoid epidemic guests are assured that all vegetables are boiled in water **PASSED BY** the manager.

If you are satisfactory, tell all your friend. If you are unsatisfactory, **WARN** the waitress.

Bathers are reminded that they must be FULLY DRESSED on **ENTRY INTO** the swimming pools and FULLY DRESSED on **LEAVING** the swimming pools.

Persons are requested not to OCCUPY SEATS in this cafe if they do not wish to **CONSUME** them.

Sports jackets may be worn, but **NEVER TROUSERS**.

And finally, here are some of
MY FAVOURITES:

Advertisement in a
NEWSPAPER:

'ENGLISS shorthanded typist. EFFICIEN.

Useless. Apply otherwise.'

Advertisement for an
BUS COMPANY:

'The comfort in our buses is NEXT TO NONE.'

Driving instructions:

'At a police-controlled crossing, drivers wishing

to turn right should wait for the all-clear before

RUNNING OVER the policeman.'

CHAPTER 9
COME INTO THE LIBRARY

Welcome to the **library**.

We have got some

GOOD JOKES here.

What did the farmer say when he found a **root vegetable** on the library shelf?

'That's a **TURNIP** for the books.'

And some **BAD** jokes.

Visitor:

CAN I HAVE A LARGE FISH AND CHIPS, PLEASE?

Librarian: This is a library!

Visitor (whispers):

Sorry. Can I have a large fish and chips, please?

You are not allowed to make too much noise in a library. If you do, you may hear the librarian call out, **'QUIET, PLEASE!'** That explains the answer to this riddle:

Q: What is a librarian's FAVOURITE **vegetable**?

A: QUIET PEAS!

In this library, we have jokes about books by authors you may have heard of, like Leo Tolstoy, who wrote *WAR AND PEACE*, and Mark Twain who wrote *THE ADVENTURES OF TOM SAWYER* and *THE ADVENTURES OF HUCKLEBERRY FINN*, and J. K. Rowling, who wrote the *HARRY POTTER* series.

What's a rabbit's favourite novel?

Warren Peace.

What did people call Tom Sawyer's friend after he **LOST A LOT OF WEIGHT**?

Huckleberry THIN.

What did the comedian say to Harry Potter?

'Why so SIRIUS?'

We have got some **brilliant books** on the shelves, too. They're by authors you may not have heard of yet.

Carpet Fitting by Walter Wall

Better Gardening by Anita Lawn

Tilling the Soil by Rosa Cabbages

Tightrope Walking by Betty Falls

The Plumber's Handbook by Lee King

Off to Market by Tobias A. Pigg

Modern Science by Alec Tricity

Haircare by Dan Druff

Rush-Hour Travel by Stan Dinroomonly

Luxury Travel by Ira Carr

On Vacation by Holly Day

Visiting the Southern United States by Louise Yanner

Travel to the Pole by Anne Tarctica

Kittens Galore! by Claude Sofa

Wearing Hats by Sonia Head

Is it Love? by Fred Itisnt

Festive Fare by Mary Christmas

Who Killed Cock Robin? by Howard I. Know

Feeding Dogs by Norah Bone

Selling Fish by Hal E. Butt

Chemistry Class by Tess Tubes

The Crime Chronicles by Robin Banks

My Dear Watson by L. M. N. Tree

Investigating Ghosts by Denise R. Knocking

Visiting the Dentist by Hugo First

Dental Surgery by Phil McAvity

A Trip to the Dentist by Yin Pain

The Bartender by Phyllis Glass

The Mix-up by Chris Cross

Household Repairs by Andy Mann

Rural Transport by Orson Cart

Slimming for Beginners by Lena Body

Springtime by Teresa Green

The Opera Singer by Topsy Sharp

I Win! by U. Lose

Robots by Anne Droid

Danger! by Luke Out

Come on in! by Doris Open

I Like Fish by Ann Chovie

May Flowers by April Showers

It's Unfair! by Y. Me

Falling Trees by Tim Burr

I Love Crowds by Morris Merrier

The Yellow River, by I. P. Freely

Hot Dog! by Frank Furter

Cry Wolf by Al Armist

Hypnotism by N. Tranced

Downpour! by Wayne Dwops

Sea Birds by Al Batross

Teach Me! by I. Wanda Know

I Say So! by Frank O. Pinion

Tug of War by Paul Hard

Surprised! by Omar Gosh

Good Works by Ben Evolent

Golly Gosh! by G. Whiz

It's Magic! by Sven Gali

April Fool! by Sue Prize

A Life of Plenty by E. Nuff

Mosquito Bites by Ivan Itch

My Lost Causes by Noah Veil

Grave Mistakes by Paul Bearer

Get Out There! by Sally Forth

Red Vegetables by B. Troot

Highway Travel by Dusty Rhodes

I Hit the Wall by Isadore There

Ship Mysteries by Marie Celeste

He Disappeared! by Otto Sight

I Hate Fighting by Boris Hell

I Didn't Do It! by Ivan Alibi

Without Warning by Oliver Sudden

Pain in My Body by Otis Leghurts

Desert Crossing by I. Rhoda Camel

Candle-Vaulting by Jack B. Nimble

Those Funny Dogs by Joe Kur

Wind Instruments by Tom Bone

Winning the Race by Vic Tree

Covered Walkways by R. Kade

I Need Insurance by Justin Case

Whatchamacallit! by Thingum E. Bob

Let's Do It Now! by Igor Beaver

I'm Someone Else by Ima Nonymous

He's Contagious! by Lucas Measles

The Great Escape by Freida Convict

Breaking the Law by Kermit A. Krime

Cooking Spaghetti by Al Dente

Good Housekeeping by Lottie Dust

Theft and Robbery by Andy Tover

The Lion Attacked by Claudia Armoff

I Love Mathematics by Adam Up

Exercise on Wheels by Cy Kling

Unsolved Mysteries by N. Igma

Lots of Excitement by Hugh N. Cry

String Instruments by Viola Player

In the Arctic Ocean by Isa Berg

Noise is Forbidden! by Nada Loud

Snakes of the World by Anna Conda

Artificial Clothing by Polly Esther

If I Invited Him . . . by Woody Kum

THE DAFT DICTIONARY

One of the best books in the library is our **DAFT DICTIONARY.** In a proper dictionary, you can find out what a word actually means. In our Daft Dictionary, you can find out what we **think** it means – usually because of the way it **sounds.**

Take the **FIRST WORD** in the Daft Dictionary: **aardvark.** An aardvark is an animal, and its name comes from the Afrikaans words for earth (*aarde*) and pig (*vark*). But what does 'aardvark' **SOUND LIKE** in English?' **'HARD WORK'.** So, it has a DAFT definition: 'something that makes you very tired'.

Once you start thinking about words in this way, there is no end to the number of daft definitions you can make up. You can use ENGLISH WORDS as well as FOREIGN WORDS and phrases. Take **à la carte**. This is a French phrase you will see sometimes on menus in restaurants. Its literal meaning is 'by the card', which means to order a meal from a range of available dishes listed on the menu (card). That's what À LA CARTE really means, but what does it mean if we give it a daft definition based on how it sounds? In the Daft Dictionary, *à la carte* means **'ON THE CART'**, or **'BY WHEELBARROW'**.

A

aardvark something that makes you very tired

absent-minded seem to have forgotten this one

abundance a lot of cakes jumping around to music

accord a thick piece of string

address an item of clothing

adore entrance to a house

à la carte by wheelbarrow

aloe a greeting

aperitif a set of dentures

arbour where boats moor at anchor

attack a small nail

axe say a question to someone

B

baggage an instrument for measuring bags

bandit when something has been outlawed

barometer instrument for measuring the contents of wheelbarrows

beadle an insect found in old churches

birdhouse home tweet home

bison something to wash hands in

blubber to whale

borough to gain temporary use of

boycott a cradle for male babies

bruise makes a cup of tea

C

cache hidden money

Caesar police order to arrest a woman

cannibal someone who is fed up with people

catkin feline relatives

cattle a place to keep cats

chimpanzee a flower apes like

climate what to do with a ladder

coconut someone who is mad about chocolate

code a virus that causes a runny nose

D

deign a person from Denmark

dogma a puppy's mother

drawing room a dentist's surgery

E

each a minor irritation

earwig a hairpiece with built-in hearing aid

eclipse what a gardener does to a hedge with his secateurs

e.g. what an h. e. n. lays

engineers what engines hear with

etching what a dog with fleas does

eureka an exclamation, as in 'eureka garlic!'

explain to skydive

extinct a dead skunk

eyebrow very intellectual

F

faith the part of a person you recognize

fete a garden party worse than death

fever a thing one person does to help another out

fiddlesticks used to play a violin

fission what nuclear scientists eat with their chips

fjord a Norwegian car

flattery living in an apartment

flea an insect that has gone to the dogs

foible what Aesop wrote

foolscap hat with a 'D' for 'dunce' on it

fortitude life after forty-one

foul language rude words used by chickens

G

gallows where no noose is good noose

gargoyle a treatment for a sore throat

germicide viruses that kill other viruses

good manners the noise you don't make when you drink your soup

goose a bird that grows down as it grows up

gorilla the part of a cooker that's used for making cheese on toast

gorgeous someone who eats a lot

granary where your mum's mother lives

grime that which doesn't pay

groan old enough to complain

guest thought about it

H

halo an angel's greeting

hatchet what a duck does with an egg

hatless the man who carried the world on his shoulders

hence birds that lay eggs

hermit a woman's hand

history a man's account of what happened

humbug a musical insect that doesn't know the words

I

ice cream what I do when I yell at the top of my voice

icicle a snowman's bike

icons what squirrels eat under oak trees

illegal a sick bird of prey

impale to put in a bucket

inkling a baby pen

intent on a camping holiday

in toto wearing a full ballet skirt

ire the opposite of lower

irritation watering the desert

J

jail free accommodation

jargon a missing container

jeep an inexpensive vehicle

jitterbug a nervous insect

joking what happens when you gag too much

joust merely

Juno Do you have any idea?

K

karma the vehicle mothers drive

kayak confection baked for birthdays and Christmas

kernel the nut in charge of a regiment

khaki device that unlocks a vehicle's door

kidnap a baby's after-lunch snooze

kidney the joint in a child's leg

kindred to dislike one's relations

kinship a boat shared with family

kipper a person who spends their time asleep

knowledge shelf on which reference books are kept

L

lapse where a cat sleeps when you're seated

lattice a green salad vegetable

launch the meal you have after take-off

lawsuit uniform worn by a police officer

ledger someone who rents a room in a house

lemming a type of fruit that can be made into a drink

lesson what someone has when they are sunbathing

lice things that provide illumination

lobster a cricketing term for a bad bowler

logarithm lumberjacks' dance

malady polite term of address for a woman

manse belonging to a man

mayor a female horse

melancholy an unhappy sheepdog

mews a poetic cat

millennium an insect with a thousand legs

mince sweets with holes in the middle

moonbeams what holds the moon up

moose a Scottish mouse

mower a bit extra

napkin when all the family's asleep

nautical bad behaviour on a boat

necks coming immediately after

Nicholas not wearing any underwear

nightingale a stormy evening

nom de plume called a feather

normalize good vision

noose what we read in the noosepapers

octopus a cat with eight legs

ode indebted

offal really bad

ohm a place to live

operetta employee of a telephone company

ouch sound made by two porcupines kissing

P

pail how you look before you kick the bucket

paradox two doctors

pas de deux the father of twins

pasteurize beyond what you can see

peace green vegetables eaten with fish and chips

phlox a number of sheep

pitcher what you draw in an art class

Q

quack an unqualified doctor who treats sick ducks

R

radish the colour of beetroot

ramshackle a chain used to tie up a
male sheep

raven going mad

rebate to put another piece of cheese in
the mousetrap

refuse what to do when the lights go out

relief what trees do in spring

research look for something a second time

rhubarb embarrassed celery

riot something not made by two wrongs

robin a thieving bird

rosette Rose had a meal

S

selfish what a fishmonger does

shamrock imitation stone

sonata a contradiction ('it's not a . . .')

spider she was seen

T

table d'hôte the table's on fire

tangent a man with a suntan

toboggan to argue to get the price down

tortoise what our teacher did

trigonometry being married to three people at once

trowel what a gardener uses to dry himself

U

udder not this one

unaware the clothing you put on first

uninhibited a place where no people live

unit a term of abuse

urchin the lower part of a girl's face

V

vesper the quiet way to talk in church

vestry a room where vests are kept

vicious kind regards, as in 'best vicious'

vicious circle a round geometrical shape with a nasty temper

viper a snake that keeps the windscreen clean

vixen a vicar's son

wade to pause for a moment

wan pale because lonely

water thirst aid

werewolf a kind of fur coat

wick seven days

wind past tense of 'win'

winsome to be lucky in a competition

winnow the part of the house you see out of

witchcraft a flying broomstick

wombat a bat with which to play wom

X what hens lay

Xenophon an ancient Greek telephone

X-ray the late Raymond

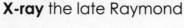

year what you hear with

youth to employ for a purpose

zinc a part of the kitchen fittings

zing what to do with a zong

zzub the noise made by a bee flying backwards

CHAPTER 10
VERSE AND WORSE!

I'm fairly GRACIOUS to the **bore**

Who tells me JOKES I've heard **before**

But he will find me GLUM and **grim**

Who tells me JOKES I told to **him**!

I once wrote the SHORTEST POEM in the history of English literature, and I like to think it is **funny**:

Ode to a GOLDFISH

O,

Wet

Pet!

I **love** poems, especially really SILLY ones. These RIDICULOUS rhymes aren't really jokes, but they are silly enough to make me **laugh**.

When in trouble, when in DOUBT,
Run in circles, scream and **SHOUT**!

ALGY met a **bear**;
The BEAR met **Algy**.
The BEAR was **bulgy**;
The **bulge** was ALGY.

It's easy enough to be PLEASANT,

When life goes ROUND and **ROUND**.

But the one worthwhile

Is the one who can **smile**

With their trousers **FALLING DOWN**.

I eat my **PEAS** with **honey**,

I've done it all my life.

It makes the peas taste **FUNNY**,

But it **KEEPS** them on the KNIFE!

If I were a **furry bear**,

And had a furry tummy,

I'd **CLIMB** into a honey jar

And make my TUMMY YUMMY!

I am a **DOG**

And you are a FLOWER,

I lift my **LEG UP**

And give you a SHOWER.

ROSES are **red**.

VIOLETS are **blue**.

Most poems RHYME . . .

but this one **DOESN'T**!

NAUGHTY
NURSERY
RHYMES

Little **JACK HORNER**

Sat in the CORNER,

Eating his **Christmas pie**.

He put in his THUMB,

But instead of a PLUM,

He **squirted** fruit juice in his **EYE**.

Do you REMEMBER this nursery rhyme?

MARY had a LITTLE **lamb**,

Its fleece was white as **SNOW**,

And everywhere that MARY went,

The LAMB was sure **TO GO**.

There are other wonderfully **silly** VERSIONS
of this rhyme, too.

MARY had a LITTLE **lamb**,

Its fleece was black as **SOOT**,

And into Mary's BREAD and JAM

Its **SOOTY FOOT** it put.

MARY had a LITTLE **lamb** –

You've heard this tale **BEFORE**.

But did you know she passed her plate

And had a LITTLE **MORE?**

MARY had a LITTLE **lamb**,

She ate it with **MINT SAUCE**,

And everywhere that MARY went,

The LAMB went, too, **OF COURSE**.

LOONY LIMERICKS

LIMERICKS are verses of **FIVE LINES**, where the **THIRD** and **FOURTH** lines are usually half the length of the first, second and fifth lines. The first limericks appeared in books published **200 YEARS AGO**, in the 1820s, but it was **Edward Lear** who made them really popular with the publication of his *Book of Nonsense* **in 1846**.

Lear, who lived from 1812 to 1888, was an ARTIST as well as a **POET**, and he was employed by the Earl of Derby to illustrate a book about the earl's **PRIVATE ZOO**. While Lear was staying with Lord Derby, he wrote **nonsense rhymes** to amuse his host's grandchildren. It was these poems that formed the basis of the *Book of Nonsense*.

Lear's limericks usually **repeated** part of the FIRST LINE in the LAST LINE.

There was an OLD MAN with a **beard**,
Who said, 'It is just as I **feared**!
TWO OWLS and a **HEN**,
FOUR LARKS and a **WREN**,
Have all built their NESTS in my **beard**!'

There was an OLD PERSON of **Dean**,
Who dined on one PEA, and one **bean**;
For he said, 'More than **THAT**,
Would make me too **FAT**,'
That cautious OLD PERSON of **Dean**.

But limericks with DIFFERENT LAST LINES are usually funnier.

An ELDERLY MAN called **Keith**,
Mislaid his set of FALSE **teeth** –
They'd been laid on a **CHAIR**,
He'd forgot they were **THERE**,
Sat down, and was BITTEN **beneath**.

There was a YOUNG MAN from **Dealing**,
Who caught the BUS for **Ealing**.
It said on the **DOOR**,
'DON'T SPIT on the **FLOOR**,'
So he JUMPED up and SPAT on the **ceiling**.

I'm PAPERING walls in the **loo**,
And QUITE FRANKLY I haven't a **clue**;
For the PATTERN'S all **WRONG**
(Or the PAPER'S too **LONG**)
And I'm STUCK to the toilet with **glue**.

There was an ODD FELLOW named **Gus**,

When travelling HE MADE such a **fuss**.

He was BANNED from the **TRAIN**,

NOT ALLOWED on a **PLANE**,

And now travels ONLY by **bus**.

There once was a FARMER from **Leeds**,

Who SWALLOWED a packet of **seeds**.

It soon came to **PASS**,

He was covered with **GRASS**,

But has all the TOMATOES he **needs**.

There was a YOUNG LADY of **Lynn**,

Who was so excessively **thin**,

That when she **ASSAYED**,

To drink **LEMONADE**,

She SLIPPED through the STRAW and fell **in**.

A PAINTER, who lived in **Great Britain**,

Interrupted TWO GIRLS with their **knitting**,

He said with a **SIGH**,

'That park bench . . . **WELL I**,

Just painted it, right where you're **sitting**.'

There was a YOUNG SCHOOLBOY of **Rye**,

Who was baked BY MISTAKE in a **pie**.

To his mother's **DISGUST**,

He emerged through the **CRUST**,

And exclaimed with a yawn, **'Where am I?'**

A young GOURMET dining at **Crewe**,

Found a rather LARGE MOUSE in his **stew**.

Said the waiter, 'Don't **SHOUT**,

And wave it **ABOUT**,

Or the rest will be wanting one, **too**.'

An ambitious YOUNG FELLOW named **Matt**,

Tried to PARACHUTE using his **hat**.

Folks below looked so **SMALL**,

As he started to **FALL**,

Then got BIGGER and BIGGER and –

SPLAT!

There was a YOUNG LADY of **Kent**,

Whose NOSE was most awfully **bent**.

She followed her **NOSE**,

One day, **I SUPPOSE**,

And no one knows WHICH WAY she **went**.

A CIRCUS PERFORMER named **Brian**,

Once SMILED as he rode on a **lion**.

They came back from the **RIDE**,

But with Brian **INSIDE**,

And the smile ON THE FACE of the **lion**.

A JOVIAL FELLOW named **Packer**,

Pulled out a JOKE from a **cracker**.

It said, 'If you're **STUCK**

For a turkey, try **DUCK** –

You could say,

"It's A REAL Christmas **quacker**!"'

An elephant SLEPT in his **bunk**,

And in slumber his chest ROSE and **sunk**.

But he SNORED – how he **SNORED**!

All the other beasts **ROARED**,

So his wife TIED A KNOT in his **trunk**.

A PROFESSOR named **Adelaide Brett**
Said, 'THREE THINGS I always **forget**.
There's all my friends' **NAMES**,
And the times of my **TRAINS**,
And the THIRD THING I don't recall **yet**.'

There was a YOUNG LADY named **Perkins**,
Who was awfully FOND of **gherkins**.
One day for her **TEA**,
She ate **FIFTY-THREE**,
And pickled her INTERNAL **workings**.

There was a YOUNG LADY named **Rose**,
Who had a BIG WART on her **nose**.
When she had it **REMOVED**,
Her appearance **IMPROVED**,
But her glasses SLIPPED DOWN to her **toes**.

There was an OLD MAN from **Milan**,

Whose LIMERICKS never would **scan**.

When told this was **SO**,

He said, 'Yes, **I KNOW**.

But I always try to get as MANY SYLLABLES

into the last line as I possibly **can**.'

There was a young man from **Peru**,

Whose limericks stopped at line **two**.

CHAPTER 11
SCHOOL
JOKES

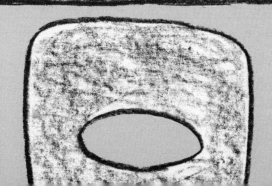

IN CLASS TODAY, we are beginning with a simple Q and A. **'Q'** stands for QUESTION and **'A'** stands for ANSWER.

Q: What's the **WORST THING** you're likely to find in the school **CAFETERIA?**

A: The FOOD!

Q: Why did the **MUSIC TEACHER** need a **LADDER?**

A: To reach the HIGH NOTES.

Q: Why did **NOSE** not want to go to SCHOOL?

A: He was tired of getting PICKED ON!

Q: What did the **GHOST TEACHER** say to the class?

A: Look at the board and I will GO THROUGH it again.

Q: Why did the teacher WRITE on the **WINDOW?**

A: Because she wanted the LESSON to be CLEAR!

Q: Why did the **TEACHER** wear SUNGLASSES?

A: Because her CLASS was so BRIGHT!

Q: Why did the teacher TURN the **LIGHTS ON?**

A: Because her class was so DIM.

Q: Why were the teacher's **EYES CROSSED?**

A: Because he COULDN'T control his PUPILS!

Q: How did the **MUSIC TEACHER** get **LOCKED** in the classroom?

A: His KEYS were inside the PIANO!

Q: What do **ELVES** learn in **SCHOOL?**

A: The ELF-ABET!

Q: Which **OBJECT** is **KING** of the classroom?

A: The RULER!

Q: What did the **PENCIL SHARPENER** say to the **PENCIL?**

A: 'Stop going ROUND IN CIRCLES and get to the POINT!'

Q: Why did the CLOCK in the school **CAFETERIA** run slow?

A: It always went BACK FOUR SECONDS.

Q: Why **DIDN'T** the sun need to go to **UNIVERSITY?**

A: Because it already has a MILLION DEGREES!

And here are some recently **OVERHEARD COMIC** classroom conversations:

TEACHER: This is the THIRD TIME I've had to tell you off this week. What have you got to say about that?

STUDENT: Thank goodness IT'S FRIDAY!

TEACHER: Mia, your figures are so bad that the eight LOOKS LIKE a three.

STUDENT: It is a three, miss.

TEACHER: Then why does it LOOK LIKE an eight?

TEACHER: Didn't you **HEAR ME** call you?

STUDENT: Yes, but you said NOT to answer back.

TEACHER: I hope **I DIDN'T SEE** you looking at Harry's exam?

STUDENT: I hope YOU DIDN'T either.

TEACHER: Didn't I tell you to STAND at the **END OF THE LINE?**

STUDENT: I tried, but there was SOMEONE ALREADY there.

TEACHER: If five people gave you £20, what do you get?

STUDENT: A NEW BIKE.

TEACHER: Say a sentence beginning with '**I**'.

STUDENT: I is –

TEACHER: Stop there, you need to begin with '**I AM**'.

STUDENT: OK . . . I AM THE NINTH LETTER of the alphabet.

TEACHER: If I had six oranges in **ONE HAND** and seven apples in the **OTHER**, what would I have?

STUDENT: BIG HANDS!

TEACHER: Answer my question **AT ONCE**, Amy. What is seven plus two?

STUDENT: AT ONCE!

TEACHER: You **MISSED** school yesterday, didn't you?

STUDENT: Not really.

STUDENT: You're **DRIVING ME CRAZY**, miss.

TEACHER: Why is that?

STUDENT: Yesterday you told us that FIVE IS FOUR PLUS ONE. Today you're telling us that FIVE IS THREE PLUS TWO!

TEACHER: What was the **ROMANS'** most remarkable **ACHIEVEMENT**?

STUDENT: Learning Latin.

TEACHER: Why were the DARK AGES so called?

STUDENT: Because they had so many KNIGHTS.

TEACHER: Tom, how do you spell 'ELEPHANT'?

STUDENT: E-l-i-f-a-n-t.

TEACHER: That's **NOT** how the dictionary spells it.

STUDENT: You DIDN'T ASK ME how the dictionary spells it.

TEACHER: I asked you to draw a COW EATING GRASS, but you've only drawn the cow.

STUDENT: Yes, miss – because the cow ATE **ALL** THE GRASS!

TEACHER: You **CAN'T SLEEP** in my class!

STUDENT: If you DIDN'T SPEAK so loudly I could.

TEACHER: What is the **SHORTEST** month?

STUDENT: May. It only has THREE LETTERS.

TEACHER: You should have been here at NINE O'CLOCK, Jane.

STUDENT: Why, what happened?

TEACHER: I wish you'd PAY A LITTLE ATTENTION to what I'm saying.

STUDENT: I'm paying as LITTLE AS I CAN.

TEACHER: Where are the ANDES?

STUDENT: At the END of the ARMIES?

TEACHER: Why aren't you doing well in HISTORY?

STUDENT: Because you keep asking me about things that happened BEFORE I was born!

TEACHER: If you had £2.75 in ONE POCKET and £5.75 in the OTHER, what would you have?

STUDENT: Someone else's trousers.

TEACHER: What is an ATOM?

STUDENT: A man who lived in the Garden of Eden with Eve?

TEACHER: If I cut THREE ORANGES and FOUR BANANAS into TEN PIECES each, what would I have?

STUDENT: A FRUIT SALAD.

TEACHER: When was **ROME BUILT**?

STUDENT: At NIGHT.

TEACHER: Why do you say that?

STUDENT: Because Rome WASN'T BUILT IN A **DAY**.

TEACHER: Use the word 'FASCINATE' in a sentence.

STUDENT: My raincoat has ten buttons but I can only FASTEN EIGHT.

TEACHER: Where do **FLEAS** go in WINTER?

STUDENT: Search me!

TEACHER: If we breathe **OXYGEN** in the DAYTIME, what do we breathe at NIGHT?

STUDENT: Nitrogen?

TEACHER: Which month has **TWENTY-EIGHT** days in it?

STUDENT: ALL of them!

TEACHER: You're new here, aren't you? What's your name?

STUDENT: Martin Mickey Smith.

TEACHER: I'll call you **MARTIN SMITH** then.

STUDENT: My dad won't like that.

TEACHER: Why is that?

STUDENT: He doesn't like people TAKING THE MICKEY out of my name.

TEACHER: Why can't you **EVER ANSWER** any of my questions?

STUDENT: Well, if I could there wouldn't be much point in me being here.

STUDENT: I used to TAKE THE BUS to school every day.

TEACHER: Why don't you any more?

STUDENT: My mother made me TAKE IT BACK every night.

TEACHER: BE QUIET until I've finished explaining! Every time I open my mouth **SOME IDIOT** STARTS TALKING.

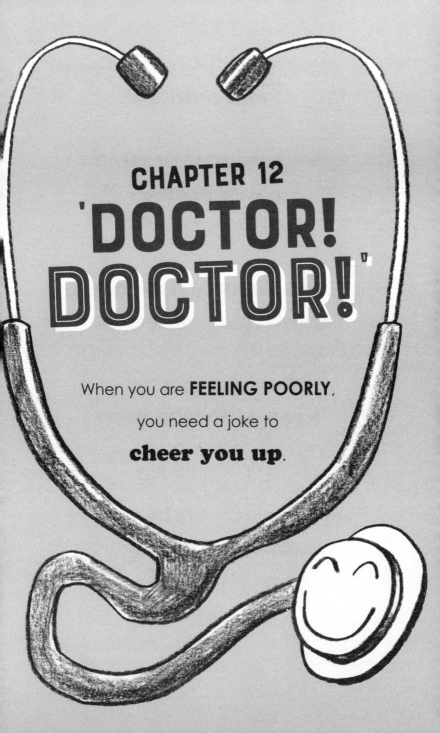

CHAPTER 12

'DOCTOR! DOCTOR!'

When you are **FEELING POORLY**,

you need a joke to

cheer you up.

Why did the **COMPUTER** go to the **doctor**?

It had a VIRUS.

Why did the **LOAF OF BREAD**

go to the **doctor**?

It was feeling CRUMMY.

Why did the **BANANA** go to the **doctor**?

Because it wasn't PEELING well.

Does an **APPLE A DAY**

keep the **DOCTOR AWAY**?

Only if you AIM it well enough.

Why did the doctor **walk past** the

medicine cupboard so QUIETLY?

So she didn't WAKE the sleeping pills.

As a rule, the best (and worst) **MEDICAL JOKES** involve **doctors** and their **patients** talking to one another. In some jokes, the DOCTOR SPEAKS **FIRST**.

'You need GLASSES.'

'How can you tell?'

'I could tell as soon as you **WALKED THROUGH** the window.'

'Did you drink your medicine **after** your bath?'

*'After drinking the bath,
I DIDN'T HAVE ROOM for the medicine.'*

'Have your eyes ever been **CHECKED**?'

'No, they've always been BLUE.'

'How did you get that **splinter** IN YOUR FINGER?'

'I scratched my head.'

But in the very best medical jokes, the **PATIENT** always **SPEAKS FIRST** – beginning with the words **'Doctor, doctor'**.

'Doctor, doctor,
I keep thinking I'm a PAIR OF CURTAINS.'
'PULL YOURSELF together.'

'Doctor, doctor, I think I'm a BELL.'
'Well, take these pills and if it's not better soon, GIVE ME A RING.'

'Doctor, doctor, I think I'm a BRIDGE.'
'What's COME OVER you?'
'So far, two cars, a lorry and a double-decker bus.'

'Doctor, doctor,
I keep thinking I'm a PAIR OF WIGWAMS.'
'Your problem is you're TOO TENSE.'

'Doctor, doctor, I think I'm a SPOON.'

'Sit still and don't STIR.'

'Doctor, doctor,

I keep thinking I'm a DUSTBIN.'

'Don't talk RUBBISH.'

'Doctor, doctor, I have the urge

to cover myself in GOLD PAINT.'

'You're suffering from a GILT COMPLEX.'

'Doctor, doctor, the OINTMENT

you gave me makes my LEG SMART.'

'Try RUBBING some on YOUR HEAD, then.'

'Doctor, doctor,

I feel like a TEN-POUND NOTE.'

'Go shopping – THE CHANGE

will do you good.'

'Doctor, doctor,

I CAN'T get to sleep at night.'

'Lie on the edge of the bed and

you'll soon DROP OFF.'

'Doctor, doctor,

can you cure my RUNNING NOSE?'

'I can give you a TAP on it.'

'Doctor, doctor,

I feel like a PACK OF CARDS.'

'Wait over there, I'll deal with you later.'

'Doctor, doctor, I'm so unhappy.

NOBODY EVER NOTICES ME.'

'NEXT!'

'Doctor, doctor,

if I take these pills, will I get better?'

'Well, no one has ever COME BACK for more.'

'**Doctor, doctor**, I feel DIZZY for HALF AN HOUR after I get up every morning.'

'*Try getting up HALF AN HOUR LATER.*'

'**Doctor, doctor**, I keep thinking I'm INVISIBLE.'

'*WHO SAID THAT?*'

'**Doctor, doctor**, I feel like a CARROT.'

'*Don't get yourself in a STEW.*'

'**Doctor, doctor**, I'm at DEATH'S DOOR!'

'*Don't worry, we'll soon pull you through.*'

'**Doctor, doctor**, I'm SHRINKING.'

'*What?*'

'I'm getting SHORTER and SHORTER!'

'*Well, just wait there and be a LITTLE PATIENT.*'

'**Doctor, doctor**, every time I drink a cup of tea I get a STABBING PAIN in my EYE.'

'*Try taking the SPOON OUT first.*'

'**Doctor, doctor**, I feel like a SHEEP.'

'*That's not so BAAAAAAAD. So do I.*'

'**Doctor, doctor**, I think I need GLASSES.'

'*You certainly do. This is the FISH-AND-CHIP SHOP.*'

'**Doctor, doctor**, what can I do? EVERYONE THINKS I'M A LIAR.'

'*I find that very hard to BELIEVE.*'

'**Doctor, doctor**, what can you give me for THE WIND?'

'*Here, try this KITE.*'

'Doctor, doctor,

they've DROPPED me from the cricket team – they called me **BUTTERFINGERS**.'

'Don't worry, what you have is NOT CATCHING.'

'Doctor, doctor,

I've only got FIFTY-NINE seconds to live.'

'HOLD ON A MINUTE, will you?'

'Doctor, doctor, I've LOST MY MEMORY.'

'When did this happen?'

'WHEN did WHAT happen?'

'Doctor, doctor,

I've gone all **CRUMBLY**, like a CHEESE BISCUIT.'

'You're CRACKERS.'

'Doctor, doctor,

I SNORE SO LOUDLY that I keep myself awake.'

'Sleep in ANOTHER ROOM, then.'

'Doctor, doctor,
can I have a SECOND OPINION?'
'Of course, COME BACK TOMORROW!'

'Doctor, doctor,
my NOSE RUNS and my FEET SMELL.'
'I'm afraid you've been built UPSIDE DOWN.'

'Doctor, doctor,
I've broken my arm in TWO PLACES.'
'I advise you not to go back to
EITHER of those places again.'

'Doctor, doctor,
I keep thinking I'M A DOG.'
'Sit on the sofa and we'll talk about it.'
'But I'm NOT ALLOWED on the sofa.'

'Doctor, doctor,

I've got a STRAWBERRY stuck in my ear.'

'Don't worry, I've got some CREAM for that.'

'Doctor, doctor,

I've SWALLOWED a fish bone.'

'Are you CHOKING?'

'No, I'm DEADLY SERIOUS.'

'Doctor, doctor,

will this ointment CLEAR UP my SPOTS?'

'I never make RASH promises.'

'Doctor, doctor,

I keep seeing SPOTS BEFORE MY EYES.'

'Have you ALREADY seen a doctor?'

'No, JUST SPOTS.'

'Doctor, doctor,

I keep thinking I'm **A MOTH**.'

'A moth?'

'Yes, a moth.'

'You need to see a PSYCHIATRIST, not a doctor.'

**'I know, but I was walking past and
I saw your LIGHT WAS ON.'**

'Doctor, doctor, when I press with
my finger HERE . . . IT HURTS, and HERE . . .
IT HURTS, and HERE . . . and HERE . . .
What do you think is wrong with me?'

'You have a BROKEN FINGER.'

'Doctor, doctor, I've got AMNESIA.'

'Just go home and try to FORGET about it.'

'Doctor, doctor, you have to help me OUT.'

'Certainly. WHICH WAY did you come in?'

'**Doctor**, **doctor**, have you got something for a **BAD HEADACHE?**'
'*Of course. Just take this HAMMER and hit yourself on the head. Then you'll have a bad headache.*'

'**Doctor**, **doctor**, my hair keeps falling out. Have you got anything to **KEEP IT IN?**'
'*How about a cardboard box?*'

'**Doctor**, **doctor**, will I be able to play the violin **AFTER** the operation?'
'*Yes, of course.*'
'That's great. **I NEVER COULD BEFORE.**'

'**Doctor**, **doctor**, I keep seeing an **INSECT SPINNING** all over the place.'
'*Don't worry, it's just a BUG that's going around.*'

'Doctor, doctor,

I can't help thinking I'm a **GOAT.'**

'Really? How long have you felt like this?'

'Since I was a KID.'

'Doctor, doctor,

I keep thinking I'm a **CATERPILLAR.'**

'Don't worry, you'll soon CHANGE.'

'Doctor, doctor, I feel like a PARROT.

Doctor, doctor, I feel like a PARROT.

Doctor, doctor, I feel like a PARROT . . .'

'Doctor, doctor,

I've got **BROCCOLI** stuck in my ear.'

'You need to eat more sensibly.'

'And I've a little bit of LETTUCE

sticking out of my other ear.'

'Yes, I see. I'm sorry to say it looks to me

like just the TIP OF THE ICEBERG.'

CHAPTER 13
MONSTER
FUN

Welcome to the weird and wonderful world of **MONSTERS**. It's a bit frightening here, so you can skip this chapter if you're someone who gets **SCARED** easily.

BOO!

STILL HERE?

Good. Now, try to stay calm as

we enter the spooktacular world of

monsters, ghosts, **PHANTOMS,**
spirits, GHOULS, poltergeists,
GOBLINS, witches, **zombies,**
mummies, WEREWOLVES
and **vampires.**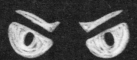

To help you out, here are some

rather **FRIGHTENING** definitions

before we get started . . .

What's a MONSTER?

An **IMAGINARY CREATURE** that is ugly, frightening or large (or all three!).

What's a GHOST?

An apparition of a **DEAD PERSON**. Also called a PHANTOM, SPIRIT or SPOOK.

What's a GHOUL?

An evil spirit or phantom. A ghoul's favourite hobby is **ROBBING GRAVES**.

What's a POLTERGEIST?

A ghost or other supernatural being that makes **LOUD NOISES** and **THROWS THINGS** about.

What's a GOBLIN?

A creature that's always getting into **MISCHIEF**. Goblins are often small, ugly and up to no good.

What's a WITCH?

Someone with **MAGICAL POWERS**, especially **EVIL ONES**. Witches wear black cloaks and pointed hats, and they fly on broomsticks.

What's WITCHCRAFT?

MAGIC and **SPELLS** performed by witches.

What's a ZOMBIE?

A **CORPSE** that has been brought back to life by witchcraft.

What's a MUMMY?

The body of a human (or animal) that has been **PRESERVED** and wrapped in bandages.

What's a WEREWOLF?

A person who changes into a wolf by the light of a **FULL MOON**.

What's a VAMPIRE?

Vampires are **UNDEAD**. They leave their graves at night to drink the blood of the living by biting their necks with **LONG FANGS**. Sometimes, vampires take the form of bats. Vampires are also said to fear garlic. To destroy a vampire, you have to pierce its heart with a wooden stake. Dracula is a **FAMOUS** vampire.

Who was FRANKENSTEIN?

Victor Frankenstein was a young doctor in a story written by the British author Mary Shelley. Dr Frankenstein created a **HIDEOUS** monster who had no name, but people sometimes call the monster he created Frankenstein.

What's HALLOWEEN?

The night of 31 October, the eve of **ALL SAINTS' DAY**, when ghosts and spirits are said to rise from the dead.

HAHA!

SOME PEOPLE celebrate **Halloween** by dressing up in **FRIGHTENING** masks and costumes and telling JOKES, like these . . .

For **Halloween**, we dressed up as almonds.
Everyone thought we were **NUTS**.

Why did the **monster** knit herself THREE socks?
Because she had THREE FEET.

Why do **ghosts** like to ride on ESCALATORS?
Because it RAISES THEIR SPIRITS!

How does a **ghoul** begin a letter?
'TOMB it may concern.'

Why did the **skeleton** miss the
HALLOWEEN PARTY?
Because he had NO BODY to go with.

Why are **graveyards** noisy?
Because of all the COFFIN!

Why don't **mummies** take HOLIDAYS?

*They're afraid that if they did,
they'd RELAX AND UNWIND!*

What is a **vampire's** favourite type of SHIP?
A BLOOD VESSEL.

What's a **ghost's** favourite DESSERT?
ICE CREAM!

Where do FASHIONABLE **ghosts** SHOP?
BOO-tiques.

What do you call a **witch**

who lives at the BEACH?

A SAND-WITCH.

What do you get when you cross

a **vampire** with a SNOWMAN?

FROSTBITE.

What kind of KEY does a **ghost**

use to unlock his room?

A SPOO-KEY.

What do you get when you cross

a **werewolf** with a **vampire**?

A FUR COAT that FANGS round your neck.

What do **ghosts** EAT FOR SUPPER?

SPOOKETI.

What does a vampire NEVER

order at a restaurant?

A STAKE sandwich.

How does a monster tell its FUTURE?

It reads its HORRORSCOPE.

Why are ghosts so bad at LYING?

Because you can see right THROUGH them!

What do ghosts use to WASH THEIR HAIR?

ShamBOO!

Who does Dracula get LETTERS from?

His FANG club.

What do skeletons say before

they begin DINING?

BONE appétit!

What happens when a ghost gets LOST in the FOG?

He is MIST.

Why don't ANGRY witches ride broomsticks?

They're afraid of FLYING OFF THE HANDLE.

How are vampires like FALSE TEETH?

Both come OUT at night.

What's the problem with twin witches?

You never know which WITCH is WHICH.

What should you do when fifty zombies surround your house?

Hope that it's Halloween.

Where do ghosts buy their FOOD?

At the GHOST-ERY store!

What's a **ghoul's** favourite

FLAVOUR of drink?

Lemon and SLIME.

What's it like to be KISSED by a vampire?

It's a PAIN IN THE NECK.

What do you call a **ghost** with a **BROKEN LEG?**

A HOBBLIN' goblin.

What do you call a **fat pumpkin?**

A PLUMPkin.

What's a **monster's** favourite **PLAY?**

Romeo and GHOULIET.

What is a **vampire's** favourite

ICE-CREAM FLAVOUR?

VEINILLA.

Who did the **monster**
take to the HORROR FILM?

His GHOUL friend.

What do you call a CHICKEN
that **haunts** people?

A POULTRY-geist.

What do **witches** put on their HAIR?

SCARE spray.

Where do **ghosts** go for a SWIM?

The DEAD Sea.

Why do **mummies** have so much
trouble KEEPING FRIENDS?

They're too WRAPPED UP in themselves.

What is a **ghost's** favourite PARTY GAME?

Hide-and-SHRIEK.

Who is the **BRIGHTEST monster?**

FRANKENshine.

Which **vampire** always eats **JUNK FOOD?**

SNACKula.

Why was the **mummy** so **TENSE?**

He was all WOUND UP.

What **tree-monster** prowls the **FOREST?**

FrankenPINE.

Which **monster** NEVER LOSES at card games?

DracuLUCK.

What do **monsters** use to
KEEP COOL in the summer?

The SCARE conditioner.

What did the critics say about

Frankenstein's OIL PAINTING?

'It's a MONSTERpiece.'

Do monsters eat popcorn WITH their fingers?

No, they eat the FINGERS SEPARATELY.

What's a monster's favourite kind of BEAN?

HUMAN BEANS.

Why wasn't there any food left after the

monster Halloween party?

Everyone there was A-GOBLIN.

What's a monster's favourite position

on the FOOTBALL TEAM?

GHOULIE.

What do you say when you

LEAVE a two-headed monster?

'BYE, BYE.'

Why did the **monster** EAT THE TORCH?

Because he wanted a LIGHT SNACK.

What kind of **horse** does a MONSTER RIDE?

A night MARE.

What kind of **monster** has the BEST HEARING?

The EARIEST one.

What kind of **vampire** does **DANGEROUS SOMERSAULTS**?

An acroBAT.

What did the **mummy detective** say when he **FIGURED OUT** the case?

'It's time to WRAP UP this mystery.'

How do **monsters** like their EGGS?

TERROR-fried.

What is a **monster's** favourite SUMMER DRINK?

DEMONade.

What kind of **monster** has TWO MOUTHS?

The kind with TWO HEADS.

When does a **monster** eat BREAKFAST?

In the MOANING.

What do **mummies** like

listening to on HALLOWEEN?

WRAP music!

What's a **ghost's** favourite PLANT?

Bam-BOO!

Why are there FENCES round **graveyards**?

Because people are DYING TO GET IN.

Why don't **ghosts** like RAIN on Halloween?

It DAMPENS their SPIRITS

Two monsters went to a **Halloween** party.

Suddenly, one said to the other,

'A lady just **ROLLED HER EYES** at me.

What should I do?'

His friend responded, 'Be a gentleman

and **ROLL THEM BACK** to her.'

Why does **Dracula** love the CIRCUS?

He always goes for the JUGGLER!

Why are **vampires** so easy to fool?

Because they're SUCKERS.

What do you call a KIND

and CONSIDERATE **monster**?

A COMPLETE FAILURE.

What do you get when you

cross a **vampire** with a TEACHER?

Lots of BLOOD TESTS!

And to finish with, a **shaggy-ghost** story . . .

One Halloween, a newspaper photographer went to a **HAUNTED CASTLE**, determined to get a photo of a **ghost**. The ghost he met turned out to be really friendly and happily posed for a few pictures. It was **MIDNIGHT** and very **DARK**, but the **PHOTOGRAPHER** had a camera with a flash. He was very pleased with the photographs he had taken – until he got them back to his office. There, he uploaded them and found that every picture was a **COMPLETE BLANK**.

The MORAL of the story?
The **spirit** was **WILLING**, but the **FLASH** was WEAK.

CHAPTER 14
SILLY RIDDLES

We have had lots of ridiculous riddles already.

These are even sillier.

What are the strongest days of the week?

Saturday and Sunday, because all the rest are WEAK days!

When is a blue schoolbook not a blue schoolbook?

When it is read!

What do you call a snail with no shell?

A slug.

When is the best time to buy budgies?

When they're going cheap.

Why don't football players get hot?

Because of all their fans!

Why did the square and the triangle go to the gym?

To stay in shape!

Why did the cow pack his bags?

Because he was MOOving!

What did the traffic light say to the car?

'Don't look. I'm changing!'

Why did the leopard refuse to take a bath?

It didn't want to come out spotless.

How was the snow globe feeling?

A little shaken!

What happens if you call 666 for the police?

The police car comes to you upside down!

What do you call a sleeping bull?

A BULL-dozer.

Why did the telephone go to the jewellery store?

It wanted a new ring.

What has four wheels and flies?

The lorry that collects the rubbish.

Why do hairdressers always get to where they're going faster than other people?

Because they know all the shortcuts.

What did one calculator say to the other calculator?

'You can count on me!'

Why is the letter 'T' like an island?

Because it is in the middle of water.

Which pillar is not used in a building?

A caterpillar.

What is the best way to catch a squirrel?

Act like a nut.

Which four letters frighten a thief?

O I C U!

Why was six afraid of seven?

Because 7 8 9!

What question can a person ask all day long, getting a different answer each time, yet all the answers are correct?

What time is it?

Why are teddy bears never hungry?

Because they're always stuffed.

What do you call a grandfather clock?

An old timer!

Why do cows wear bells?

Because their horns don't work!

What happened when the wheel was invented?

It caused a revolution!

What do librarians take with them when they go fishing?

Bookworms.

What is the world's tallest building?

The library, because it has the most stories.

What kind of running means walking?

Running out of fuel.

What do you get if you cross a

cow and a duck?

A creamy quacker!

What's red and mushy and is found

between a shark's teeth?

Slow swimmers.

Where will you find the biggest rope

in the world?

In EuROPE!

What do bananas do when they get a sunburn?

They peel.

Why do cats always go after mice and birds?

Because cats like fast food.

How do you start a teddy-bear race?

You say, 'Ready, teddy, go!'

What did the paper say to the pencil?

'You are looking very sharp today.'

What does a polar bear use to keep his head warm?

A polar ice cap.

How can we tell that carrots are good for our eyes?

Have you ever seen a rabbit wearing glasses?

If frozen water is iced water, what is frozen ink?

Iced ink! (Don't worry. You don't really.)

RIDDLES OFF
THE TOP OF
YOUR HEAD

What do you call a man with a spade on his head?

Doug.

What do you call a man without a spade on his head?

Douglas.

What do you call a man with a plank on his head?

Edward. (As in 'head-wood'!)

What do you call a woman with two toilets on her head?

Lulu.

What do you call a woman with a cat on her head?

Kitty.

What do you call a man with a seagull on his head?

Cliff.

What do you call a man with a paper bag

on his head?

Russell.

What do you call a man with a black

smudge on his head?

Mark.

What do you call a woman with a Christmas

tree on her head?

Carol.

What do you call a man with a bag of

soil on his head?

Pete (as in 'peat').

What do you call a man with a number

plate on his head?

Reg.

What do you call a man with a walking stick on his head?

Cain.

What do you call a woman with an oyster on her head?

Pearl.

What do you call a man with very short hair on his head?

Sean (as in 'shorn', meaning cut short).

What do you call a man wearing a notice on his head that says, 'The End'?

Saul (as in 'that's all!').

FOOL A FRIEND

To round off our riddles, here are some trick ones for you to try out on your friends.

YOU: Ask me if I'm a cat.

FRIEND: Are you a cat?

YOU: Yes. Now ask me if I'm a dog.

FRIEND: Are you a dog?

YOU: No, stupid. I just told you I'm a cat!

YOU: Would you hit somebody after they had surrendered?

FRIEND: No.

Now you can (gently!) hit your friend and announce: 'I surrender!'

YOU: How do you keep a fool in suspense?

FRIEND: I don't know. How do you keep a fool in suspense?

YOU: I'll tell you next week.

YOU: Look at that henweigh in the garden!

FRIEND: What's a henweigh?

YOU: About 3 pounds.

YOU: You'd better keep your eyes open tomorrow.

FRIEND: Why?

YOU: You'll bump into something if you don't.

YOU: What is red and goes ding-a-ling?

FRIEND: A red ding-a-ling.

YOU: What is green and goes ding-a-ling?

FRIEND: A green ding-a-ling.

YOU: What is yellow and goes ding-a-ling?

FRIEND: A yellow ding-a-ling.

YOU: What is orange and goes ding-a-ling?

FRIEND: An orange ding-a-ling.

YOU: No, you're wrong. They don't make them in that colour.

YOU: What has six legs and barks at strangers?

FRIEND: I don't know.

YOU: A dog.

FRIEND: A dog?

YOU: I gave it two extra legs to make it harder.

YOU: Will you remember me in fifty years?

FRIEND: Yes.

YOU: Will you remember me in twenty years?

FRIEND: Yes.

YOU: Will you remember me in ten years?

FRIEND: Yes.

YOU: Will you remember me in five years?

FRIEND: Yes.

YOU: Will you remember me next year?

FRIEND: Yes.

YOU: Will you remember me next month?

FRIEND: Yes.

YOU: Will you remember me next week?

FRIEND: Yes.

YOU: Will you remember me tomorrow?

FRIEND: Yes.

YOU: Will you remember me in an hour's time?

FRIEND: Yes.

YOU: Will you remember me in a minute's time?

FRIEND: Yes.

YOU: Will you remember me in a second's time?

FRIEND: Yes.

YOU: Knock, knock!

FRIEND: Who's there?

YOU: You've forgotten me already.

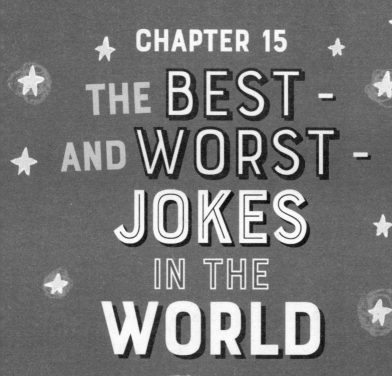

CHAPTER 15

THE BEST –
AND WORST –
JOKES
IN THE
WORLD

AT LAST!

HERE THEY ARE:

the one hundred best –

and worst – jokes in the world.

WELCOME TO THE

COMEDY

COUNTDOWN!

100. What did the **DRUMMER**

call his TWIN DAUGHTERS?

Anna ONE, Anna TWO!

99. What does a BABY COMPUTER

call his **FATHER**?

DATA!

98. A man just attacked me with MILK,

CREAM and BUTTER. **HOW DAIRY!**

97. I asked my FRENCH friend if she likes to

play VIDEO GAMES. She said, **'WII.'**

96. I wondered why the FRISBEE was

getting **BIGGER**. Then it **HIT ME**.

95. Becoming a VEGETARIAN is a

big **MISSED STEAK**.

94. Don't interrupt someone working intently on a **PUZZLE**. Chances are, you'll hear some **CROSSWORDS**.

93. 'I thought you were going **WATERSKIING**.'
'*I was, but I couldn't find a SLOPING LAKE.*'

92. 'Police in Manchester are looking for a bloke with **ONE EYE** called **GERALD**.'
'*What's his OTHER EYE called?*'

91. DAD: Ben, why do you have a **BLACK EYE**?
BEN: I bruised TWO FINGERS knocking in a nail in the carpentry class.
DAD: But your fingers look all right and that **DOESN'T EXPLAIN** your black eye.
BEN: Oh, yes, it does.
THEY **WEREN'T** MY FINGERS.

90. CUSTOMER: A pound of steak, please, and make it **LEAN**.

BUTCHER: Certainly, sir. WHICH WAY?

89. TOM: This match **WON'T** light.

TAM: That's funny. IT DID THIS MORNING.

88. JULIE: How do you spell **'ERBERT**?

DAD: You mean **HERBERT**, don't you?

JULIE: No, 'erbert. I've written the H down already.

87. DARREN: Mum, can I go **OUT** and **PLAY**?

MUM: What, in THOSE CLOTHES?

DARREN: No, in the **PARK**.

86. DON'T TRUST **ATOMS**.

They MAKE UP everything.

85. My girlfriend told me she was leaving me because I keep pretending to be a TRANSFORMER. I said, 'No, wait! **I CAN CHANGE**.'

84. I've decided to sell my **HOOVER** . . . It was just collecting **DUST**.

83. A book just F_{ELL} on my head. I've only got **MY SHELF** to blame.

82. I was interrogated over the THEFT of a **CHEESE TOASTIE**. They really **GRILLED** me.

81. I'm reading a book about ANTIGRAVITY. It's impossible to **PUT** D_{OWN}.

80. I wasn't originally going to get a BRAIN TRANSPLANT, but then **I CHANGED MY MIND**.

79. I had a job TYING sausages together, but I couldn't make **ENDS MEET**.

78. My new girlfriend works at the ZOO. I think she's a **KEEPER**.

77. My landlord says he needs to come and talk to me about how HIGH my **HEATING BILL** is. I told him, 'My door is always OPEN.'

76. I used to build STAIRS for a living. Business was **UP** and **DOWN**.

75. I'm friends with TWENTY-FIVE LETTERS of the alphabet. I DON'T KNOW **WHY**.

74. Does anyone need an ARK? **I NOAH GUY!**

73. Why did **CINDERELLA** get

KICKED OFF the football team?

Because she kept

RUNNING FROM THE BALL!

72. What's at the BOTTOM of
the ocean and SHIVERS?
A NERVOUS WRECK!

71. What's the difference between a
WELL-DRESSED man on a **UNICYCLE** and
a POORLY DRESSED man on a **BICYCLE**?
*AT**TIRE**!*

70. Why did the COFFEE go
to the **POLICE STATION**?
It got MUGGED.

69. What did the **GRAPE** do
when he got STEPPED on?
He let out a LITTLE WINE.

68. How does a **PENGUIN** BUILD its house?
IGLOOS it together.

67. I used to work in a SHOE-RECYCLING SHOP.

It was **SOLE DESTROYING**.

66. I saw an advert in a window that said:

'Television for sale, £1, VOLUME STUCK ON FULL.'

I thought, 'I CAN'T TURN THAT **DOWN**.'

65. The **SHOVEL** was a

GROUNDBREAKING invention.

64. What do you call a person in a **TREE**

with a **BRIEFCASE** and a **LAPTOP**?

A BRANCH MANAGER.

63. What did the FRIED RICE say to the **SHRIMP**?

Don't WOK away from me!

62. Local man KILLED by FALLING piano.

It will be a **LOW KEY** funeral.

61. The last thing Grandpa said **BEFORE** he KICKED THE BUCKET?

'HOW FAR do you think I can kick this bucket?'

60. How do you make a Swiss **ROLL**?

Push him off the top of an Alp.

59. JUDGE: Constable, do you **RECOGNIZE** this woman?

POLICE OFFICER: Yes, m'lud. She approached me when I was in plain clothes and tried to pass this **TWENTY-POUND NOTE** off on me.

JUDGE: **COUNTERFEIT?**

POLICE OFFICER: Yes, m'lud. SHE HAD TWO.

58. What do you feed to **BABY GNOMES** to make them GROW big and strong?

ELF-RAISING flour.

57. Which king of England invented the **FIREPLACE**?

Alfred the GRATE.

56. How do you make **GOLD SOUP**?

Put FOURTEEN CARROTS in it.

55. Did you hear about those new **REVERSIBLE JACKETS**? I'm excited to see how they **TURN OUT**.

54. Did you hear about the two **SILK WORMS** in a race? It ended in a **TIE**!

53. Thanks for explaining the word **'MANY'** to me. **IT MEANS A LOT.**

52. Who has a **PARROT** that shouts,

'Pieces of four! Pieces of four!'?

SHORT John Silver.

51. What did the **EARWIG** say as

it fell out of the **WINDOW?**

''ERE WE GO!'

50. What did one **CATERPILLAR** say to

another when it saw a **BUTTERFLY?**

'You'd NEVER GET ME UP

in one of those things!'

49. What's YELLOW, BROWN and **HAIRY?**

Cheese on toast DROPPED on the CARPET.

48. What do you call **TWO SPIDERS**

who have just got **MARRIED?**

Newly WEBS.

47. A Spanish magician was doing a magic trick. He said, 'UNO, DOS . . .' and then he disappeared without a **TRACE**.

46. Did you hear about the PESSIMIST who hates GERMAN SAUSAGE? He always fears the **WURST**.

45. I've written a song about **TORTILLAS**. Actually, it's more of a **RAP**.

44. The person who invented the DOOR KNOCKER won the **NOBEL** Prize.

43. I was at the **CLIMBING CENTRE** the other day, but someone had stolen all the grips from the wall. **YOU COULDN'T MAKE IT UP!**

42. I own a pencil that used to be owned by WILLIAM SHAKESPEARE, but he chewed it a lot. Now I can't tell if it's **2B** or **NOT 2B**.

41. LONG fairy tales have a tendency to **DRAG-ON.**

40. A patient was admitted to hospital with **EIGHT PLASTIC HORSES** in his stomach. His condition is **STABLE**.

39. I found a rock that measured 1,760 YARDS in length. Must be some kind of **MILESTONE**.

38. What do you call a factory that sells **PASSABLE PRODUCTS**?

A SATISfactory!

37. Why did the **INVISIBLE MAN** TURN DOWN the job offer?

He couldn't SEE HIMSELF doing it.

36. What's the difference between a **TENNIS BALL** and the PRINCE OF WALES?

One is HEIR TO THE THRONE and the other is THROWN INTO THE AIR.

35. Two **ANTENNAE** met on a roof,

fell in love and got married.

The ceremony wasn't much,

but the **RECEPTION** was excellent.

34. I went to buy some **CAMOUFLAGE**

TROUSERS the other day, but

I COULDN'T FIND ANY.

33. What did one **OCEAN** say to

the other **OCEAN**?

Nothing, they just WAVED!

32. What do you call a **BOOMERANG**

that DOESN'T come back?

A STICK!

31. Did you hear about the

ITALIAN CHEF WHO DIED? He **PASTA** way.

30. LULU: Do you like my new SWIMMING POOL?

MO: It's beautiful. But why

isn't there any water in it?

LULU: I CAN'T swim.

29. I was hoping to STEAL SOME LEFTOVERS

from the party, but my plans were **FOILED**.

28. Most people are **SHOCKED** when they find

out how BAD AN ELECTRICIAN I am.

27. Some CLOWN opened the door for me

this morning. That was a nice **JESTER**.

26. I don't trust **STAIRCASES**.

They're always UP to something.

25. The first time I got a REMOTE CONTROL for the TV, I thought, 'This **CHANGES** everything.'

24. MO: Do you believe in **COINCIDENCES**?

LULU: That's amazing. I was about to ask you the SAME QUESTION.

23. I got fired from the CANDLE factory because I refused to work **WICK ENDS**!

22. Police have ARRESTED the world **TONGUE-TWISTING** champion. I imagine he'll be given a tough **SENTENCE**.

21. What do you call someone with **NO BODY** and **NO NOSE**?

Nobody KNOWS!

20. What do you call a
CAN OPENER that doesn't work?
A CAN'T opener!

19. How many tickles does it
take to **TICKLE** an **OCTOPUS**?
TENTACLES!

18. I just watched a documentary about
BEAVERS. It was the best **DAM** show I ever saw!

17. You know what the **LOUDEST** pet
you can get is? A **TRUMPET**.

16. Why did the **SCARECROW** WIN an award?
He was OUTSTANDING IN HIS FIELD.

15. A **HAM SANDWICH** walks into

a bar and orders a beer.

The bartender says,

'Sorry, we DON'T SERVE FOOD here.'

14. When is a **DOOR** NOT A DOOR?

When it's AJAR.

13. Why can't you HEAR a

PTERODACTYL when it goes to the toilet?

Because the PEE IS SILENT!

12. What do you call a

man who **CAN'T STAND**?

NEIL.

11. I used to have a job at a **CALENDAR FACTORY** but I got the SACK because I **TOOK** a couple of days OFF.

10. Did you hear about the **TWO THIEVES** who STOLE A CALENDAR? They each got **SIX MONTHS**.

9. I'm **TERRIFIED** of **LIFTS**. I'm going to start taking **STEPS** to avoid them.

8. What's the BEST PART about living in **SWITZERLAND**? *I don't know, but the FLAG IS A BIG PLUS.*

7. Don't worry if you MISS a gym session. Everything will **WORK OUT**.

6. Ever tried to **EAT A CLOCK**? Don't.

It's TIME-CONSUMING.

5. What toy goes DOWN

but doesn't come UP?

A YO.

4. Why are **COLDS** such BAD ROBBERS?

Because they're so EASY TO CATCH.

3. Why are **CATS** BAD STORYTELLERS?

Because they only have ONE TALE.

2. How do you organize

a SPACE-THEMED **PARTY**?

You PLANET.

1. What does the **QUEEN**

do when she **BURPS**?

She issues a ROYAL **PARDON**!

That's it. I was going to end with a vegetable
joke, but it's too corny, so that's your lot.

ONE LAST TRICK

Take a piece of paper and write the word **'WHAT'** on it. Put the piece of paper in your pocket. Now find a friend and say to your friend, 'I know what you are going to say next.' Your friend will ask, **'WHAT?'** You can then produce your piece of paper from your pocket and say, 'I told you I knew what you were going to say next!'

ONE LAST POEM

There once was a LADY from **GLOUCESTER**,

Whose parents thought they had LOST **HER**.

From the FRIDGE came a **SOUND**,

And AT LAST she was **FOUND**.

The problem was how to **DEFROST HER**!

ONE LAST RIDDLE

What do you call a **NICE** lumberjack?

A DECENT FELLER!

ONE LAST JOKE

Cuthbert noticed his neighbour Egbert looking at something in the front garden.

'Lost something, Egbert?' he asked.

'Yes,' said Egbert. 'My spectacles.'

'Where did you last see them?' asked Cuthbert.

'In the living room,' replied Egbert.

'Then why are you looking for them out here?' asked Cuthbert.

'There's more light out here,' said Egbert brightly.

ONE MORE RIDDLE?

Oh, all right.

Why did the boy call his DOG SANDWICH?

Because he was HALF-BRED!

ONE MORE?

How do you find a LOST RABBIT?

Make a NOISE like a CARROT!

ONE MORE?
NO!

GO ON
How should you DRESS on a VERY COLD DAY?

Quickly!

Why did the FISH BLUSH?

Because the sea WEED!

Who TRACKS down LOST VICARS?

The Bureau of MISSING PARSONS!

How was SPAGHETTI invented?

Someone used their NOODLE!

**What's the difference between Gyles,
the Joke Bloke, and an umbrella?**

You can SHUT UP an umbrella!

STOP!

If you say so.

What did the SATISFIED CUSTOMER say
after they'd finished their copy of *What's Black
and White and Red All Over?* The **Best
Worst** Joke Book in the **WORLD**?

Turn the page to **find out**.

HELLO.

Are YOU still HERE?

You shouldn't be. This is the end of the book. What? You want to start all over again? With *more* 'knock, knock' jokes? That's where we came in, isn't it?

Well, if you insist . . .

Knock, knock!

Who's there?

A little old lady.

A little old lady who?

I didn't know you could yodel.

Knock, knock!

Who's there?

Willy.

Willy who?

Willy or won't he?

Knock, knock!

Who's there?

Justin.

Justin who?

Justin time for tea.

Knock, knock!

Who's there?

Sonia.

Sonia who?

Sonia shoe – I can smell it from here!

Knock, knock!

Who's there?

Olga.

Olga who?

Olga home if you don't open up!

Knock, knock!

Who's there?

Les.

Les who?

Les go out and have some fun!

Knock, knock!

Who's there?

Watson.

Watson who?

Watson your mind?

Knock, knock!

Who's there?

Ida.

Ida who?

Ida nice friend before I met you.

Knock, knock!

Who's there?

Michael.

Michael who?

Mike'll go away if you don't let him in.

Knock, knock!

Who's there?

Harriet.

Harriet who?

Harriet all my sandwiches.

Knock, knock!

Who's there?

Roland.

Roland who?

Roland butter, please. I'm feeling peckish.

Knock, knock!

Who's there?

Renata.

Renata who?

Renata sugar. Can I borrow some?

Knock, knock!

Who's there?

Felix.

Felix who?

Felix my ice cream, I'll wallop him!

Knock, knock!

Who's there?

Canoe.

Canoe who?

Canoe help me with my homework?

Knock, knock!

Who's there?

Thistle.

Thistle who?

Thistle be the last time I knock on your door!

Knock, knock!

Who's there?

Cook.

Cook who?

Oh, that's the first cuckoo I've heard this year!

Knock, knock!

Who's there?

Noise.

Noise who?

Noise to see you!

Knock, knock!

Who's there?

You.

You who?

You who, is there anybody there?

Knock, knock!

Who's there?

Esther.

Esther who?

Esther anything I can do for you?

Knock, knock!

Who's there?

Don.

Don who?

Don' mess about – open the door!

Knock, knock!

Who's there?

Willoughby.

Willoughby who?

Willoughby quick and open the door!

Knock, knock!

Who's there?

Boo.

Boo who?

Oh, don't start crying again!

Knock, knock!

Who's there?

Sacha.

Sacha who?

Sacha lot of questions!

Knock, knock!

Who's there?

Dinosaur.

Dinosaur who?

Dinosaurs don't go, 'Who,' they go, 'ROAR!'

Knock, knock!

Who's there?

The interrupting cow.

The interrupting cow wh–

Moo!

Knock, knock!

Who's there?

Hacienda.

Hacienda who?

Hacienda the book. It really is.

IT **REALLY** IS.

GYLES BRANDRETH is the WORLD'S leading collector of JOKES.

He has also featured in the *Guinness Book of Records* for speaking **NON-STOP** for twelve and a half hours. He has appeared on **lots** of TV programmes, including *The One Show, Gogglebox, Pointless, Mastermind, Countdown, The Chase, Tipping Point, The IT Crowd, QI* and *Have I Got News for You.* On radio, he is a regular on *Just a Minute* and on stage he has appeared in **EVERYTHING** from Shakespeare to pantomime. Oh, yes, he has! (He once appeared in Shakespeare's most famous play, *Hamlet.* It was not a success. The audience threw **EGGS** at him. He went on as Hamlet; he came off as omelette.)

Once the Member of Parliament for the city of Chester, he is now chancellor of the University of Chester. As well as writing lots of books and collecting jokes and riddles, Gyles collects **TEDDY BEARS**. They all live in the Brandreth Bear House at Newby Hall, near Ripon in North Yorkshire.

Gyles lives in London with his wife, three children, seven grandchildren and the neighbour's cat, Nala.

Website: gylesbrandreth.net
Twitter: @GylesB1
Instagram: @gylesbrandreth